Plays for Children

A Collection of Noteworthy Non-Royalty Plays

Volume 1

**Plays By
Theodora DuBois
Lloyd Bradey
Louise Saunders
A. A. Milne
Marguerite Merington
E. Harcourt Williams
Wadeeha Atiyeh**

Edited by James Geisel

**Children's Theatre Plays
Theatre Arts Press**

Plays for Children

NOTE: This plays in this collection may be performed without a royalty, however the making of copies from this book is strictly prohibited.

For more information on producing these plays, to purchase individual cast copies, and for a list of titles published, visit:

Childrens-Theatre-Plays.com

Copyright © 2015 Theatre Arts Press

All rights reserved. No part of this publication may be reproduced or transmitted in any form or by any means, now known or yet be to invented, electronic or mechanical, including photocopy, recording, or any information storage and retrieval system.

This book or any portion thereof may not be reproduced or used in any manner whatsoever without the express written permission of the publisher except for the use of brief quotations in a book review or scholarly journal.

Special discounts are available on quantity purchases by educators. For details, contact the publisher at theatreartspress.com.

Printed in the United States of America
9 8 7 6 5 4 3 2 1

Contents

ALADDIN 5
    by Theodora DuBois

DICK WHITTINGTON 49
    by Lloyd Bradey

THE PRINCESS AND THE WOODCUTTER 87
    by A. A. Milne

THE KNAVE OF HEARTS 101
    by Louise Saunders

CINDERELLA 123
    by Marguerite Merington

SNOW-WHITE AND ROSE-RED 147
    by E. Harcourt Williams

ALI BABA 157
    by Wadeeha Atiyeh

Plays for Children

Plays for Children

ALADDIN

by **Theodora DuBois**

Characters

Aladdin
Zobeid, his mother
Abdalla, his uncle
Tunkah, his aunt
Jullanar, his friend
Princess Badroulbadour
An Old Man
The Magician
Genie
Sultan
Grand Vizier
Servants of the Sultan, Guards, Citizens of Cathay

ACT ONE
Scene 1
A street in old Cathay

Scene 2
In the Magic Cavern

Scene 3
Zobeida's house

ACT TWO
Scene 1
The Sultan's audience room in the grand palace

Scene 2
The Court of Aladdin's Palace.

Scene 3
The street in Cathay

Scene 4
The Court of Aladdin's Palace

ACT ONE
Scene 1

A street in old Cathay, late afternoon.

The lights rise upon an empty stage. Enter ZOBEIDA, carrying a gorgeous coat which she has been embroidering, TUNKAH, carrying a basket, and ABDALLA, carrying a string of shoes. They toddle in a row with little short steps. When they reach the center of the stage, they face the audience, and call:

ZOBEIDA, TUNKAH, ABDALLA. Aladdin! Aladdin! Aladdin!!

(There is silence.)

ABDALLA. *(To audience.)* Ho, people of the market place, has anyone seen Aladdin?

JULLANAR. *(From the back of the audience.)* Yes, I have seen Aladdin.

(She runs down through the audience and climbs up on to the stage.)

ABDALLA. Well, where is he? He was to take these shoes I have finished making to the Grand Vizier.

TUNKAH. No, he is to take this basket to Hung Chow, the mandarin —

ZOBEIDA. He was to take this coat to the Sultan's palace.

ZOBEIDA, TUNKAH, ABDALLA. *(To JULLANAR.)* Where is Aladdin? What is he doing?

JULLANAR. He is flying kites from the great wall.

ZOBEIDA. Oh, did you ever know such a bad boy!

Plays for Children

TUNKAH. Such a naughty, wicked, lazy, bad, bad, bad boy!

ABDALLA. To fly kites!

ABDALLA. To fly kites on the great wall!

ZOBEIDA. He might fall off.

JULLANAR. There were lots of boys. Their kites were fighting way up in the air. Aladdin's was the best kite. His was beating the others. It swooped and dashed around in the air as if it were a live thing. Aladdin shouted songs at it.

ZOBEIDA. Oh, did you ever know such a silly boy!

TUNKAH. Shouting songs at kites!

ABDALLA. Such a silly, silly, foolish boy.

ZOBEIDA. Oh, whatever shall I do with Aladdin? He sings songs and plays and dances all day long. Whatever shall I do with Aladdin?

TUNKAH. He says he will not grow up to be a tailor like his father.

ABDALLA. Ah — his good father, Mustapha the tailor, who is dead. Aladdin runs the streets all day.

TUNKAH. And dances.

ZOBEIDA. And sings. — Don't you think, sister, he has a voice like a nightingale, a little?

TUNKAH. How foolish you are about your son Aladdin.

ABDALLA. Yes, how ridiculous you are about your son Aladdin.

TUNKAH. He wastes his time all day.

ABDALLA. And runs after the Sultan's elephants.

TUNKAH. And the Princess Badroulbadour's palanquin —

ABDALLA. Yes, I have often seen him, in the dusk, running after the Princess' golden palanquin.

JULLANAR. Here come slaves now bearing the Princess home from the baths.

> *(A tom-tom is heard offstage. It grows nearer. Then down the center aisle goes a procession, led by the GRAND VIZIER. A golden dosed canopy is carried. Populace and children follow. ALADDIN, carrying a large kite, is the last. He runs and catches up with the palanquin as the slaves carry it up on the stage. Just as it reaches the center of the stage, ALADDIN comes to its side. The curtains part, the PRINCES looks out and drops a flower in ALADDIN'S hand. He kneels, bowing his head low to the PRINCESS.*

7

Plays for Children

The procession passes by, and goes out. ZOBEIDA, TUNKAH, and ABDALLA have been bowing and nodding at one side during all the passing of the procession. JULLANAR has followed procession out.)

ABDALLA. *(As sound of the tom-tom dies away.)* There is Aladdin now!

ZOBEIDA. Oh, my darling boy, you didn't fall off the wall!

ABDALLA. Come here, you rascal. You never finished those shoes I left you mending this morning.

TUNKAH. You never finished this basket; you put it on your head and danced around like a dervish!

(They try to get hold of ALADDIN but he dances impishly away from them, singing.)

ALADDIN. Oh, I'll not make baskets and I'll not make shoes,
You can chase me till you tumble down, for I'll be a prince.
And I'll have a throne, in a palace on the edge of the town.
I'll not make coats and I'll not make shoes,
You can chase me till your old brain whirls.
My palace will be of emeralds,
Diamonds, rubies, amber, pearls —

(The tom-tom is heard offstage and ALADDIN pulls ZOBEIDA, ABDALLA, and TUNKAH offstage saying:)

ALADDIN. Come, the Princess again. Come, come —

(They go out. The OLD MAN enters, struggling with a great armful of wood. Some of it slips from his grasp and as he bends to pick it up he drops more and cannot seem to get it all together again. JULLANAR enters, and jeers at the OLD MAN.)

JULLANAR. *(Hopping up and down.)* Ho, ho, old stupid stork. Stupid stork — stupid stork. Dropped his sticks and couldn't walk!

OLD MAN. *(Pitifully.)* Don't laugh at me. — Oh, the demons are in you.

(He gets his sticks together and staggers on. JULLANAR, impishly up behind him, pulls a stick out of his bundle. They fall again. OLD MAN groans and JULLANAR laughs. ALADDIN enters, left, in time to see what she has done. He pulls her angrily away as she is about to repeat the trick.)

ALADDIN. *(Angrily.)* Shame, Jullanar, shame — to tease an old man.

JULLANAR. *(Hopping up and down.)* Can't get me — can't get me — you slow snail — try and see.

Plays for Children

ALADDIN. *(Sternly.)* Be still, Jullanar. *(To OLD MAN.)* Let me help you. Your sticks are heavy.

(He picks them up and piles them in OLD MAN'S arms.)

JULLANAR. Not angry, Aladdin? Not angry?

ALADDIN. Yes, very angry at you, Jullanar. *(The OLD MAN sways.)* See, he is ill.

OLD MAN. No — no — only hungry. Very hungry.

ALADDIN. *(Takes a banana from his sash.)* Here, take this banana.

JULLANAR. Oh, Aladdin, you said that banana was for your supper, you have not eaten since breakfast.

ALADDIN. *(Fiercely, as the OLD MAN looks at him in doubt.)* And what have not eaten? I am young and strong. It will not hurt me to be hungry. The time will come when I shall eat hundreds of bananas! *(Grandly.)* Eat, Old Man, eat!

OLD MAN. *(Humbly.)* A prince, perhaps? *(He puts down his sticks and eats.)*

ALADDIN. Ah, I shall be a prince! Such a prince the world has ever known. Some day I shall dig far down in the earth under the mountains and there find mounds of buried treasure, glitter-diamonds and emeralds and rubies by the quart.

JULLANAR. Bring me a quart of pearls, Aladdin — I should love a ton of pearls.

ALADDIN. *(Lost in his dream.)* And I shall build a palace with bricks of gold and silver and ivory, and lattices glowing with precious stones, and I shall marry the Princess Badrouldabour, the daughter of the Sultan. Every evening, as the red sun sinks behind the great wall and the bells of the temple ring, I watch the Princess Badroulbadour returning from the baths. Four elephants she has, as white as cream, and they bear her crimson litter with its curtains of golden silk. I steal out from the street side and run beside her elephants. And from her litter comes a scent of musk and roses and jasmine, and a hand, white as the moon, parts the golden curtains and drops me a flower through the curtains.

(There is a pause.)

OLD MAN. *(Scratching his head.)* I saw no elephants in the procession.

JULLANAR. Aladdin sees things that we can never see. If he says elephants, there were elephants.

OLD MAN. Elephants coming down there?

JULLANAR. *(Stamping her foot.)* Yes, yes. Why must everybody be always spoiling his beautiful stories?

OLD MAN. A mighty prince. I must carry my sticks home.

(He bends to pick up the sticks. ALADDIN rouses from his dream and helps the OLD MAN.)

ALADDIN. Let me help you. *(They go toward exit carrying sticks. ALADDIN turns back and calls softly to JULLANAR.)* Jullanar, I am breaking in two with hunger. See if you can beg a bowl of rice.

(As they are about to go out they come upon ZOBEIDA, TUNKAH, and ABDALLA who are entering.)

ABDALLA. Oh, there you are, you worthless demon. What are you doing!

TUNKAH. Stealing that poor old man's sticks, I'll be bound.

ZOBEIDA. Oh, Aladdin, how could you — how could you! You will break my heart.

OLD MAN. Thanks, Prince—

(He takes his sticks and leaves.)

ALADDIN. *(Defiantly.)* Do you think that I, a prince, would steal a beggar's sticks?

ABDALLA. *(Angrily.)* A prince, a prince he calls himself. He looks it, doesn't he? Ah, ha! — a prince of rags and tatters — a prince of kite fliers — a prince of idlers! You come and make those shoes I set you at this morning, young man.

ALADDIN. A fat old owl lived in a tree and he made people's shoes, did he — He said, "Here's a prince that's young and gay, I'll make him mend my shoes all day." But the Prince said, "Thank you, I refuse to work all day at making shoes." And the owl was angry as he could be and flew a-hooting from his tree — !

ZOBEIDA. Shame, Aladdin, shame, to call your good uncle an owl!

ABDALLA. An owl — an owl — sister, did you hear? He called me an owl, me. *(He hits himself on the chest.)* Abdalla, the best maker of shoes in all Cathay — oh, scandalous — oh, shocking —

TUNKAH. I think it's disgraceful, sister — an owl — disgraceful — I should sell that boy to the Sultan for a slave. Then he would learn to work, I can tell you. Come, brother, we will go home.

ABDALLA. Come, sister — an owl — scandalous —

(They go out.)

JULLANAR. *(Impishly, as an owl.)* Too-hoo — too-hooo — too-hoooo.

(She flaps out after them.)

ZOBEIDA. Aladdin, Aladdin, how could you!

ALADDIN. Did you hear what she said? That she would sell me to the Sultan for a slave. A slave — to work in the chalk pits and quarries like an ox. And they thought I was stealing the old man's sticks! They never understand — *(His voice is bitter. His mood has changed to somber unhappiness.)*

ZOBEIDA. You should not have called your good uncle an owl.

ALADDIN. But that is not a bad thing to call an uncle. Why was he so angry? Why does he always think everything so evil? It is not evil to fly kites from the great wall, or to sing songs and dance, or to follow the palanquin of the Princess. It makes one forget that one is cold, and tired, and poor, and hungry.

ZOBEIDA. But they cannot understand, my son.

ALADDIN. No, they cannot — I pretend to be a prince. I imagine my jewelled castle, wonderful food on golden dishes — and when I try to taste the food — it is only dreams — just empty broken dreams.

ZOBEIDA. Oh, but Aladdin, they're foolishness, your dreams. Can't you be satisfied and do what your uncle wants? Make shoes.

ALADDIN. No, Mother, I can't — it sickens me — I won't be satisfied, I won't give up my dreams. I'll fight for them. I'll go thirsty and hungry — that's nothing —

ZOBEIDA. Oh, bitterness, to have your child go hungry!

ALADDIN. *(Puts his arm around his mother.)* Mother, do you think I am so wicked and worthless?

ZOBEIDA. *(Strokes his hair.)* I think you're the best boy in all the great flat world, Aladdin.

ALADDIN. Then don't ask me to give up my dreams, Mother. They're like a lamp, shining in dark, frightening caverns. The lamp is there ahead of you, leading you, showing the way. It will lead you to do anything in the world that you want — if you keep your dreams clear and bright and shining — it will lead us, Mother, to a palace — and a princess —

ZOBEIDA. I'm sure I'd rather have it lead me to a stew of goat's meat.

Plays for Children

(The MAGICIAN comes in, and lurks in the shadows, watching ALADDIN and ZOBEIDA.)

ALADDIN. *(Laughing.)* Well, Mother — perhaps we may have a stew of goat's meat yet tonight. Give me the coat you have embroidered and I will take it up to the palace. They will give me a coin or two, perhaps.

ZOBEIDA. *(As she exits.)* They should give you a coin or two. I worked on it for days.

JULLANAR. *(Enters, not noticing the MAGICIAN, calls excitedly.)* Oh, Aladdin, Aladdin — One of the boats is burning in the river by the lower rice fields! Come and see!

ALADDIN. No, I must take this coat to the palace.

(His mother comes back with coat, and a lantern on the end of a long pole. It is deep dusk now on stage.)

JULLANAR. Oh, bother the coat! Come on. The flames of the boat leap like dragons climbing to the sky.

ALADDIN. *(Wistfully.)* I cannot come, Jullanar. Good-bye.

(He takes the coat and lantern, kisses his mother and goes out.)

ZOBEIDA. *(To JULLANAR.)* Why are you always trying to make him do what he shouldn't do? A better boy than Aladdin never lived. What other boy, I'd like to know, would go on an errand for his mother when he might be seeing a burning boat? He's the best boy in all Cathay.

(She exits.)

JULLANAR. I never said he wasn't.

(She starts to go, but is stopped by the MAGICIAN.)

MAGICIAN. Don't scream.

JULLANAR. *(Terrified.)* What is it you want? I have no jewels or money.

MAGICIAN. *(Sarcastically.)* No? I thought you were an Empress at least. Who is that boy?

JULLANAR. Aladdin.

MAGICIAN. Aladdin ?

JULLANAR. Yes, just Aladdin.

MAGICIAN. *(Musingly.)* He seems bright enough. Is he brave?

JULLANAR. Aladdin is brave as a lion.

Plays for Children

MAGICIAN. Hmm — Who is his father?

JULLANAR. Mustapha, the tailor. He is dead.

MAGICIAN. Dead. Good! What was Mustapha like, child? Tall — strong — fine looking?

JULLANAR. No, a little man, grey, like a mouse, with a scar running across his forehead.

MAGICIAN. What did he like to eat? What were his habits?

JULLANAR. How do I know? He was not my father!

MAGICIAN. *(Sternly.)* Child, if you are impudent, I shall call up the yellow demons of Iblees to curse you — the scarlet dragons of Kashmiri to eat you up.

JULLANAR. *(Terrified.)* No, no — don't — call the dragons!

MAGICIAN. Then answer my questions. What did Aladdin's father like to eat?

JULLANAR. A stew of goat's meat, I think, with curried rice and onion. Why do you want to know?

MAGICIAN. Ask me not or I will call up my dragons and they will crawl and growl before you spitting fire. Now go — and when you come again do not remember that I have ever asked you questions. Do not remember that we have met before — forget me. You will forget me?

JULLANAR. Yes, yes — if you want —

MAGICIAN. *(Waving his arms.)* Now go quickly, or my dragons will come bounding after you, spitting fire in the dark.

JULLANAR. No — no — no—

(She scurries off, looking back over her shoulder in dread. The MAGICIAN crosses away majestically, stands a moment, then calls.)

MAGICIAN. Mustapha! — Mustapha! *(He turns, looks at the audience and says:)* Can anyone in the market-place please tell me if I am near the house of Mustapha, the Tailor?

(ZOBEIDA comes in, looking very frightened.)

ZOBEIDA. I — I hear someone speaking my husband's name.

MAGICIAN. Mustapha, the Tailor?

ZOBEIDA. Mustapha, the Tailor.

MAGICIAN. Then you are Zobeida, his wife?

Plays for Children

ZOBEIDA. I am Zobeida. It is true.

MAGICIAN. My heart is a lute string of joy. A garden of delight at seeing you.

(He embraces her. She screams.)

ZOBEIDA. *(Struggling to get away.)* Oh, oh, fiend, cobra, jackal!

MAGICIAN. *(Letting her go.)* Zobeida — have I been too hasty in my joy? Have I frightened you — my sister?

ZOBEIDA. I am no sister of yours. Away — away!

MAGICIAN. Am I a hen, woman, that you flap me away with curses?

ZOBEIDA. Go away — go away !

MAGICIAN. Ask your husband, woman, if he would have his brother kicked away like a dog.

ZOBEIDA. Oh — my husband — he is dead —!

MAGICIAN. *(Recoiling, his hand to his forehead.)* Mustapha — my brother — dead!

ZOBEIDA. Aye, two years with Allah — praise be his name.

MAGICIAN. *(Overcome with grief.)* My heart is a desert of grief to learn that Mustapha, my brother, is dead.

ZOBEIDA. Mustapha had no brother.

MAGICIAN. *(Angrily.)* No brother? Who am I then, I should like to know?

ZOBEIDA. I cannot tell you.

MAGICIAN. *(Holds both hands upward as if in supplication.)* Mustapha — Mustapha! How well I remember him — so small and grey, yet noble — that great scar running across his forehead. His favorite dish of goat's stew and curried rice —

ZOBEIDA. Oh — you must be my husband's brother!

MAGICIAN. I have traveled over the whole flat world to share with him my gold.

ZOBEIDA. You are my husband's brother!

(She falls into his arms. ALADDIN enters, left, with lantern. He is singing.)

ALADDIN. "Roses, cedar wood and musk. Jasmine flowers through the dusk —" *(He stops short in amazement. ZOBEIDA and the MAGICIAN*

Plays for Children

part from the embrace. ZOBEIDA in embarrassment.) By the name of Allah —who is this man?

ZOBEIDA. Aladdin — be not angry — it is — it is —

MAGICIAN. *(Standing with folded arms.)* Who is this youth?

ALADDIN. Sir, I am Aladdin.

ZOBEIDA. Aladdin — here is your uncle.

ALADDIN. What uncle ? Can Abdalla have grown so tall and thin in an hour?

ZOBEIDA. He is your father's brother.

ALADDIN. My father had no brother.

ZOBEIDA. He has crossed the world to share with us his wealth.

ALADDIN. I would not touch his wealth with a bamboo pole.

MAGICIAN. *(Turning to go.)* Then farewell.

ZOBEIDA. No — no — brother — don't go! Aladdin has not the manners of a jackal — stay — stay —

MAGICIAN. *(Stops and turns back.)* I was lonely — I had hoped to find a son in the son of my brother. I was weary, I had hoped to find rest — I was hungry — I had hoped to find food — and you turn me out —

ALADDIN. No, stay if you are hungry, We will find you food.

(ZOBEIDA motions wildly to ALADDIN, then runs up to him.)

ZOBEIDA. *(In loud whisper.)* There is nothing to eat in the house but an old goat's bone.

ALADDIN. Here are two pennies they gave me at the Palace.

MAGICIAN. Two pennies, for this feast of joy! *(He gives a small bag, that chinks when it is shaken, to ZOBEIDA.)* Sister, let this be a banquet. Go, buy food in the market-place. Here is gold.

ZOBEIDA. *(Running off.)* I have a bag of gold — a bag of gold. Oh, they will think we have found a fortune —

MAGICIAN. *(Putting his hand on ALADDIN'S shoulder.)* My boy, you will not regret this day that you have taken me into your father's house. Let me tell you that I mean to share with you the greatest treasure that the world has ever seen.

ALADDIN. Treasure?

MAGICIAN. Yes, treasure.

Plays for Children

ALADDIN. Buried treasure?

MAGICIAN. Yes, deeply buried.

ALADDIN. Gold?

MAGICIAN. Gold, in great glittering mounds!

ALADDIN. *(As if he were seeing the treasure before him.)* Jewels?

MAGICIAN. Jewels? Heaps of them, great piles of them. Gardens of trees bearing jewels for fruits — fountains raining diamonds and emeralds.

ALADDIN. Oh, let us go there, let us see them!

MAGICIAN. I will take you tomorrow at daybreak. Out, far out beyond the barren mountains, beyond the great wall — beyond the ruined temple in the Wilderness of Djinns. *(In a low voice.)* Aladdin, are you afraid?

ALADDIN. I am afraid of nothing. *(Excitedly.)* Why must we wait until tomorrow? Let us start now.

MAGICIAN. We start tomorrow. At dawn, we seek the treasure in the Wilderness of Djinns!

(The lights fade as ALADDIN invasions the treasure with the MAGICIAN smiling behind him.)

ACT ONE
Scene 2

In the Magic Cavern.

ALADDIN is dimly seen climbing down the ladder. The MAGICIAN'S voice is heard shouting down from above the top of the ladder

MAGICIAN'S VOICE. *(Impatiently.)* Go down — go down — go down, boy —

ALADDIN. *(Maintaining self-control with difficulty.)* I am going down, my dear Uncle. Did you think I was going up?

MAGICIAN'S VOICE. There is no need to be insolent to me.

ALADDIN. Nor is there need for you to be insolent to me.

MAGICIAN. Bah — an elephant could climb more quickly.

ALADDIN. Then why did you not bring an elephant instead of me.

MAGICIAN. *(Angrily.)* You will regret your rudeness. Are you so slow because you are afraid?

(ALADDIN stands on one of the bottom rungs of the ladder and looks up.)

ALADDIN. I am slow because the ladder is old and the wood is rotten and some of the rungs are gone.

MAGICIAN. That is not true. It is as safe as the door-steps at your own home.

ALADDIN. Really? Then why have you not climbed down yourself instead of sending me?

MAGICIAN. *(Roaring.)* Insolent boy! Will you hurry and get that lamp as I told you?

ALADDIN. *(Standing at the bottom of the ladder.)* No, I will not hurry. *(He speaks calmly and politely but with an edge of sarcasm.)* I have no wish to hurry. For five days have I wandered with you in this Wilderness of Djinns, and every minute of that time have you cursed me for my laziness. When I slept you beat me with sticks to wake me up. You promised me treasure and dragged me into a desert. You tried to frighten me with spells and incantations, and then you made me hoist a flat stone, heavy as a mountain, and drove me down that rotting ladder to fetch an old brass lamp — *(Bitterly.)* That is the treasure you promised!

MAGICIAN. You will regret — you will regret —

ALADDIN. Where are the gold and jewels you promised me?

MAGICIAN. I promised nothing. For the last time, will you hurry and get that lamp?

ALADDIN. It is bad for one to hurry, Uncle — Ohhhh —

(He sees the lamp in the niche and goes toward it, in wonder.)

MAGICIAN. What is it?

ALADDIN. Your lamp. Are these fellows alive? *(He approaches the dog idols gingerly and puts a hand on the head of one.)* Good dog — good dragon — they're stone — jade — worth a king's ransom. Would that I could carry one home.

MAGICIAN. *(Impatiently.)* Touch nothing but the lamp. Touch nothing but the lamp or the walls will roll together and crush you.

ALADDIN. Really? *(He takes the lamp and holds it high above his head.)* The lamp — the lamp — !

Plays for Children

MAGICIAN. Now quickly come, bring it to me.

ALADDIN. Time enough, Uncle. There are years ahead of us. There is no need to hurry so.

(He examines the lamp.)

MAGICIAN. Hand me up the lamp.

ALADDIN. When I have come out of the cave.

MAGICIAN. Hand me the lamp, I say.

ALADDIN. When I have come out of the cave, I say.

MAGICIAN. *(Roaring horribly.)* For the last time — will you hand me that lamp?

ALADDIN. I will not!

MAGICIAN. Then stay there in that cave until the earth crumbles into the dust of empty time! May the yellow demons of Kaf creep through the crannies of the rocks and torment you — may the Djinns of Eblis —

ALADDIN. *(Shouts.)* I am not afraid. *(The trap door clangs shut above and the cave is in total darkness.)* I am not afraid — only babes and children are afraid in darkness. If you are still, and have no fear, you begin to see the darkness as light. *(Gradually the cave becomes lighter and all its glories are seen. He stands looking about him with awe and delight.)* Ohh — what gold — what jewels! Now my mother will be rich! She can have that tunic embroidered with storks and palaces! *(He goes wonderingly to chests and piles of jewels and puts handfuls of gold and jewels in his sash and inside his clothes.)* Jullanar can have new clothes — and a feast for the Old Man — and the children of the streets — and Abdalla and Tunkah, too! I shall make them rich forever. How my mother will rejoice — Oh! *(Then he stands still looking about him and realizing that he is a prisoner. He gives one gasping sob.)* No, no — I will get out — My mother — it would be too dreadfully sad for her— *(He shouts.)* Let me out! Let me out! *(Silence.)* Let me out! *(He climbs the ladder and seems to be trying to lift up a heavy weight, with no success. Then he climbs down and stands a minute looking at the lamp, and says to it.)* It is your fault that I am locked up here. No, I will not be afraid. A tarnished old lamp. All covered with spots —

(He rubs the lamp with his sleeve. There is a clash of cymbals — lights go out, come on, and the GENIE stands before ALADDIN, and bows.)

GENIE. Master, speak the words of your wish and it shall be granted.

ALADDIN. *(Amazed.)* And who, and what are you?

GENIE. I am the slave of the lamp which you hold in your hand. When you rub it, I obey your wish.

AIADDIN. Any wish?

GENHE. Yes, Master, any slightest wish.

ALADDIN. Anything at all in the world?

GENIE. Yes, Master. Master, what is your desire?

ALADDIN. Oh, I have so many wishes they crowd into my mind like a stampede of wild camels. I wish — I wish first —

GENIE. What was your desire when you rubbed the lamp?

ALADDIN. That I might be with my mother. She will be so troubled. I have been away so long, and she thinks there are demons and djinns beyond the Great Wall.

GENIE. There are. Then your wish, Master?

ALADDIN. *(Puts the lamp under his arms and claps his hands.)* Take me home — in a cloud of magic smoke!

(A clash of cymbals, smoke, darkness.)

ACT ONE
Scene 3

Zobeida's house.

When the lights rise, TUNKAH, ZOBEIDA, and ABDALLA are seen sitting on stools. ZOBEIDA in the middle, TUNKAH and ABDALLA on either side facing each other.

ABDALLA. You must not worry about Aladdin.

TUNKAH. No, sister, you must not worry about Aladdin.

ABDALLA. He is not worth worrying about.

ZOBEIDA. I am not worrying.

TUNKAH. That is right, sister.

ZOBEIOA. Why should I worry?

ABDALLA. No reason at all. How long has he been gone now?

ZOBEIDA. For five days.

TUNKAH. *(Shakes her head.)* Five days in the Wilderness of Djinns!

ABDALLA. The last caravan to cross it saw green demons fighting a dying tiger one morning in the mists of dawn.

TUNKAH. Aye, and they saw two djinns hiding in a marsh by a ruined temple.

ZOBEIDA. Oh, and my Aladdin is out there with all those demons and beasts and genies!

TUNKAH. That is all nonsense!

ABDALLA. A bad coin always comes back to its owner.

ZOBEIDA. *(Angrily.)* You call my Aladdin a bad coin! There is no one in Cathay as fine and brave and noble as my Aladdin. How dare you call my Aladdin a false coin! Out upon you!

ABDALLA. Our sister has forgotten herself, Tunkah.

(He rises.)

TUNKAH. Yes, our sister has forgotten herself.

ZOBEIDA. Yes, I have forgotten myself — my heart is breaking. Oh, think he will meet those green demons — Ayie — Ayie — Ayie!

TUNKAH. Let us go, Abdalla—until our sister has recovered herself.

ABDALLA. Yes, Tunkah, let us go.

(They go out of the door. ZOBEIDA sits on her stool rocking and sobbing in woe.)

ZOBEIDA. Oh, Aladdin — Aladdin — my son — my son —

(JULLANAR steals in the door. She comes up and looks at ZOBEIDA shyly.)

JULLANAR. *(Softly.)* Has not Aladdin come back yet?

ZOBEIDA. No, no — my heart is broken!

JULLANAR. He is all right. Surely no harm could come to so brave and fine a boy as Aladdin!

ZOBEIDA. It is always the brave and fine ones to whom harm does come.

JULLANAR. No, no!

ZOBEIDA. They go with heads held high, and a song on their lips — and we can only remember their arms about our necks — their kisses — and laughter — but it is not theirs — not their laughter that we hear — some other children laughing in the streets —

JOLIANAR. I will find him for you. I will climb one of the vines up the Great Wall and search the plains beyond. Surely I will see him coming home — singing —

ZOBEIDA. Oh, Aladdin!

(JULLANAR steals out softly. Suddenly there is a clash of cymbals, smoke, darkness, light again. ALADDIN is seen sitting cross-legged on the divan. ZOBEIDA shrieks and looks at him in astonishment. He throws back his head and laughs.)

ALADDIN. Why, Mother, you look as if you had seen a vision.

ZOBEIDA. *(Irritated.)* A vision indeed! What do you mean by rushing in like that, with all that noise and clatter? It's enough to frighten anybody out of their senses! And where have you been hiding all this time, I'd like to know? Worrying me to death! And your aunt and uncle have been frightening me with I don't know what all tales of djinns and beasts and demons beyond the Great Wall.

ALADDIN. *(Goes over to her and gives her cheek a peck-like kiss.)* But aren't you even a little glad to see me?

ZOBEIDA. *(Rubs the kiss off her cheek.)* Do you expect me to dance and clap my hands with joy like a houri?

ALADDIN. Yes, a most beautiful houri. *(Teasingly.)* Your cheeks are almond blossoms. Come, clap your hands and dance, that your son has come home.

(He makes her clap her hands.)

ZOBEIDA. *(Breaking away from him.)* Stop, stop, Aladdin. Are you shameless?

(She shakes him by the shoulder and a string of jewels fall from his coat upon the floor.)

ALADDIN. Take care, Mother.

(He picks up the jewels.)

ZOBEIDA. *(Awed.)* Oh, what are those?

ALADDIN. Rubies—and pearls — and diamonds! *(He takes strings and strings of jewels from his garments and tosses them up in the air, juggling them.)* And sapphires, and topaz, and amethyst and jade —

ZOBEIDA. *(With excitement.)* They are worth a king's ransom. Wherever did you get them?

ALADDIN. *(Dancing about.)* Don't you wish you knew? Don't you wish you knew?

Plays for Children

ZOBEIDA. Where did you?

ALADDIN. I picked them off ruby and sapphire trees, of course.

ZOBEIDA. *(Angrily.)* Don't be ridiculous.

ALADDIN. Ah, but I did — and look at these!

(He takes a bag from inside his coat and opens it. ZOBEIDA looks in.)

ZOBEIDA. Oooohhhh! What emeralds! What pearls! *(Terrified at a sudden thought.)* Aladdin, you have stolen them! Allah have mercy that I should have a thief for a son!

ALADDIN. *(Takes the lamp from his sash.)* No, Mother, I am not a thief.

ZOBEIDA. *(Snatches lamp from him.)* And what's this lamp? Oh, you have robbed some palace or a caravan. Do you know no better than that? We will be dragged off by the Sultan's guard and thrown into his snake pit. Why did you steal this worthless old lamp? All tarnished, too.

(She rubs the lamp with her sleeve and ALADDIN shouts out:)

ALADDIN. Take care!

(There is a clash of cymbals, smoke, darkness, light. The GENIE has appeared and stands, bowing, in front of ZOBEIDA.)

ZOBEIDA. *(Clings to ALADDIN and shrieks.)* Oh — Oh! Aladdin, what is it?

GENIE. I am the Genie of the Lamp.

ZOBEIDA. *(Pushes lamp into ALADDIN'S hands.)* Take it away — take it away!

ALADDIN. Why, Mother, don't be so frightened!

GENIE. What is your wish?

ZOBEIDA. Go, — go!

ALADDIN. Be careful, Mother, if you tell him to go, he will.

ZOBEIDA. All the better, all the better. What do I want with a great ugly genii bringing a lot of smoke into the house? Of course I want him…

ALADDIN. Be careful, Mother, he is the Slave of the Lamp. He will bring you anything in the world you desire.

ZOBEIDA. I don't believe it.

GENIE. What is your wish?

Plays for Children

ZOBEIDA. Well, I'll tell him a wish just to show he can't bring it. Then, perhaps, Aladdin, you'll be satisfied, and stop your fooling about— *(with disgust)*—genii and things. It's ridiculous! *(To GENIE.)* Stop all that bowing, it's nonsense.

GENIE. Yes, oh Mistress. What is your desire?

ZOBEIDA. I should like a new tunic, — a green one — embroidered with moons and peacocks and pagodas.

ALADDIN. Produce such a garment.

GENIE. *(Bowing.)* Your wish shall be obeyed.

ZOBEIDA. *(Excitedly.)* Wait a minute — wait a minute! Aladdin, do you think he could bring us something to eat?

ALADDIN. *(Grandly.)* Surely, a banquet —

ZOBEIDA. No, no, not a banquet. I would never have bowls or dishes enough for a banquet.

ALADDIN. Don't worry about bowls. *(To GENIE.)* Bring us golden bowls by the dozens.

GENIE. *(Bowing.)* Your wish shall be granted.

ZOBEIDA. No, no, stop — wait — not golden bowls by the dozens. All the thieves in Cathay would be about our doorsteps. *(To GENIE.)* Bring only three golden bowls — or four, perhaps.

ALADDIN. And what would you like for food? Peacock's breast, perhaps, or tiger steaks, or delicious, golden fried gold fish?

ZOBEIDA. No, no — how extravagant. No, I should like a bowl of cumin ragout with chicken breast fricandoed, flavored with sugar, pistachios, musk and rose water — and bring coffee, aromatic as perfume.

ALADDIN. And bring me a garment fit for a Sultan, and, hereafter, obey my wishes without yourself appearing.

GENIN. Your wishes shall be granted.

(There is a clash of cymbals, smoke, darkness, light. The GENIE has gone. On one stool is a tray laden with golden bowls, fruits, etc. Over another stool are gorgeous garments.)

ZOBEIDA. Oh, oh, oh — A-l-a-d-d-i-n!

ALADDIN. Now, do you see, Mother?

ZOBEIDA. He's done it. He's done it! Golden bowls, four of them! *(She lifts one which is used as a cover.)* Oohh — gold — what gold — as heavy

23

Plays for Children

as a stone! Smell this chicken, Aladdin! Pistachios, and the gravy, thick as butter.

ALADDIN. And see these garments, Mother!

ZOBEIDA. Oh — fit robes for the favorite wife of a Sultan!

(TUNKAH and ABDALLA enter the doorway and stand amazed.)

TUNKAH. Whatever has happened! Is Aladdin back?

ALADDIN. *(Lightly.)* No, Tunkah, no, I am flying kites from the Great Wall!

ABDALLA. Where is his uncle, Mustapha's brother?

ZOBEIDA. *(Paying no attention.)* Look, Abdalla, look! *(She holds up garments.)*

ALADDIN. Smell, Tunkah, smell! *(He brings bowl of food to TUNKAH.)*

ZOBEIDA. Look, look, all embroidered with peacocks and pagodas.

ALADDIN. Taste, taste, all flavored with musk and rose water! *(He spins about in a circle.)*

TUNKAH. What has happened? Where did they come from?

ABDALLAH. Has Aladdin married the Princess?

ALADDIN. Not yet, not yet, but very soon. *(Wraps her new garment about her. She tries to push him off.)* See how beauteous she is, Tunkah, Abdalla! A moon of joy, a passion flower of delight! *(He flings a string of jewels over TUNKAH's head.)* And these jewels, oh Tunkah, shall be yours to keep — and this gold, Abdalla! *(He pours pieces of gold into ABDALLA'S hand.)* Take this gold and with it buy a house above the rice fields.

ABDALLA. *(Pleased in spite of himself.)* It feels like gold. *(He bites a coin.)* Yes, I always knew you were a smart boy, Aladdin.

ZOBEIDA. A smart boy — a smart boy — he is a prince, my Aladdin! My heart bursts with riches!

ALADDIN. My heart bursts — my heart is a fountain that leaps to the sun. *(He grabs ZOBEIDA'S hands and TUNKAH'S, who has hold of ABDALLA. As before, ALADDIN forces them into an absurd jigging dance.)* Come, dance, dance that all this joy has come to us!

ZOBEIDA. *(Panting.)* Stop, Aladdin, stop, stop. Why, I'm all to pieces!

TUNKAH. And your dinner will be getting cold.

ABDALLA. Good food wasted while you keep us dancing here.

Plays for Children

ALADDIN. It is good to dance. It keeps the heart warm.

ABDALLA. Humph — and the chicken cold!

ALADDIN. Come, come, no harm is done. Sit and eat. *(They move bench and place stools about it.)* Now, Mother, Tunkah. *(He moves the tray of dishes.)*

ZOBEIDA. Sister, will you have some of this fricandoed chicken?

ABDALLA. The feast is good, although somewhat cold. Where, Aladdin, is your uncle, your father's brother, with whom you went into the wilderness?

ZOBEIDA. Yes, Aladdin, I declare I quite forgot him.

ALADDIN. It is best to forget him.

TUNKAH. Why, what a thing to say of your dear father's good brother!

ALADDIN. Let him be forgotten. Mother, when you have finished eating, I wish you to dress yourself in your robes and go at once to the Sultan.

ZOBEIDA. Aladdin, you are crazy.

TUNKAH. Crazy.

ABDALLA. His riches have bereft him of his wits.

ALADDIN. I am not crazy, and you must do as I say! You must take these jewels to the Sultan. *(He puts strings of jewels in one of the golden bowls.)* And tell him that you come to ask the hand of his daughter for your son in marriage.

ZOBEIDA. Why, Aladdin, you have lost your wits. He will throw me into the snake pit. Imagine my asking the Princess to marry you, the son of a tailor! He'll order his elephants to trample on me! I won't go one step —

ABDALLA. *(Mockingly.)* Now that you have a few jewels and a handful of gold, I suppose you will be saying you are a Sultan or a Caliph — ha-ha!

TUNKAH. A pretty Sultan, a tailor's son in rags!

ALADDIN. *(Rising from the table.)* Aye, mock if you wish — laugh and jeer and mock me! But you, Mother, must go to the palace of the Sultan and tell him that your son is the Caliph of Chrysophrand!

TUNKAH and **ABDALLA.** *(Laughing.)* Ha-ha! Chrysophrand! Where's that?

ALADDIN. The place where chrysophrase comes from. Now, listen. You are to go to the Sultan and say that your son has more treasure than in all the mines of Cathay: uncounted herds of elephants and a palace of ivory and porphyry and gold and chrysophrase — Mother, shall I summon the Slave of the Lamp to make you obey my wishes?

ZOBEIDA. There is no Slave of the Lamp. I dreamed him, Aladdin.

ALADDIN. He is my dream, Mother, and my dreams are more real than your reality.

ABDALLA. The Caliph of Chrysophrand! Ha-ha!

(He stuffs a large piece of chicken in his mouth and eats unpleasantly.)

ALADDIN. *(Holds the lamp high and rubs it.)* Oh, Slave of the Lamp, make these people believe my words.

(There is a clash of cymbals, and, for a minute, silence. The mood of ZOBEIDA, ABDALLA, and TUNKAH has changed into one of awe of ALADDIN. They rise from their seats and edge away from him with bows and salaaming, sincere and terrified.)

ABDALLA. *(Humbly.)* It is not fit that we sit in the presence of my exalted nephew, the Caliph of Chrysophrand.

ZOBEIDA. The Sultan should be proud to have his daughter wed my son.

TUNKAH. Speak, oh Caliph, and you will be obeyed.

ALADDIN. *(Grinning.)* Oh Magic, indeed —

ZOBEIDA. *(Taking the bowl of jewels.)* I go to the Sultan, my son.

ABDALLA. And if it be your wish, oh Caliph, I shall go with your mother to the Palace gates.

TUNKAH. And may I, too, go to the palace gates, oh Caliph of Chrysophrand?

ALADDIN. *(Raising his hand.)* You have permission to depart.

(They bow, and go out. ALADDIN takes up the new robe that he has not yet put on. Takes off his tattered jacket, puts on the new robe, and stands a moment, thinking. As he stands there, JULLANAR rushes in.)

JULLANAR. Aladdin, they told me you were back. We thought you had been carried off by genii and demons. *(He smiles, but does not answer.)* You are as serious as an old brass idol! Come, we have a fire down by the ancient temple in the rice fields. We are going to dance and sing and fly burning kites about it. Come, hurry!

Plays for Children

ALADDIN. I cannot come, Jullanar, I have other things to do.

JULLANAR. Oh, come on, we're going to play at tiger hunting.

(She takes his hand and tries to pull him. He stands still and shakes his head.)

ALADDIN. *(Sadly.)* No, Jullanar, I shall never again fly burning kites by the ancient temple in the rice fields, or play at tiger hunting in the dusk.

JULLANAR. Why, why not? What's the matter with you?

ALADDIN. Jullanar, will you do something for me?

JULLANAR. Why, of course, what is it?

ALADDIN. *(Hands her the bundle of his old tunic.)* Take this and burn it on your fire. And buy a stick or two of incense and throw them on the flames.

JULLANAR. Why, what is this? It's your old cloak!

ALADDIN. It is my youth, Jullanar.

JULLANAR. What do you mean? And what are you all dressed up for?

ALADDIN. *(Handing her pieces of gold.)* Say my farewells to my playmates — and my love! Say that I shall not forget the kite on the Great Wall, or fishing from the old junks in the river. Tell them not to forget that Aladdin was their friend.

JULLANAR. *(Heart-brokenly.)* Aladdin, where are you going?

ALADDIN. If I reach out my hand I can pluck my dreams from the Tree of Fulfillment. But will they be as fair when I hold them — will they fade? Well, I am going to marry the Princess Badroulbadour, Goodbye, Jullanar, farewell!

(He kisses her on the forehead and goes out. JULLANAR bursts into wild weeping, and flings the money he gave her on the floor. After a few moments the MAGICIAN peers in the doorway.)

MAGICIAN. *(Coming in.)* Why are you weeping?

JULLANAR. *(Alarmed.)* Where did you come from?

MAGICIAN. I, too, have magic means of transportation. Where is Aladdin?

JULLANAR. Gone to marry his Princess. I hate her, I hate her —

MAGICIAN. Shall we save him from the fatal mistake of marrying her?

JULLANAR. Yes, yes!

Plays for Children

MAGICIAN. Then let us hasten after him to the Sultan's audience room in the palace.

JULLANAR. And what shall we do there?

MAGICIAN. We shall see — then we shall see! But you must do everything I tell you to, to the last word. If you do, the Princess shall not have him. And here is that bag of gold I promised you before. Now, be silent as we go, for I must repeat spells to summon up my fiends and demons! Oh, demons of Kaf — El Asslim — Sot and Teer — in the whirlwinds of sand — in the heat of the storm — come — come —

(He waves his arms. The lights fade to black as they go out.)

End of Act One

ACT TWO
Scene 1

The SULTAN'S audience room in the grand palace. Through the windows one can see the SULTAN'S gardens.

When the lights rise the PRINCESS BADROULBADOUR is seen reclining on the divan. A SERVANT is fanning her, another SERVANT is dancing, and a third beats the cymbals in time to the music. The PRINCESS is obviously bored. She yawns once or twice, and kicks off her soft Turkish slipper at the dancing SERVANT.

PRINCESS. Stop! Stop!

DANCING SERVANT. Oh, what have I done that you should throw slippers at me!

PRINCESS. Pick it up. Bring it to me. *(The SERVANT obeys.)* I am deadly tired of the same old music, the same old dances, the same old gardens, the same old palace. *(Yawns.)* Ohh — how dull, how dull, how dull!

OTHER SERVANT. But, Princess, soon the people will come here to tell your father, the Sultan, their troubles, and to ask his favors and judgment. That is always amusing.

PRINCESS. *(Yawns again.)* Always the same old troubles to listen to — it's dull — dull! *(She kicks the slipper off her foot again and it sails high in the air.)* Bring it back.

(The SERVANT obeys.)

Plays for Children

SERVANT. But, Princess, they say there is at this moment an old woman talking to your father, the Sultan. They say she is the mother of a Caliph, and she asks your hand in marriage for her son.

PRINCESS. *(Bored.)* Always a Caliph or a King or a Sultan wanting to marry me. I should want to marry a new sort of person, a street boy sort of person, beautiful and in rags; he would run beside my palanquin at dusk, and I would drop him a jasmine flower.

SERVANT. A street boy to marry a Princess!

PRINCESS. Oh, I suppose it would be unheard of. But they might make some new laws. I hate old things. I despise them! *(She kicks her slipper off high in the air.)* Bring it back. *(The SERVANT obeys.)* And I think my father might build me a new palace of gold and silver and precious stones — *(She kicks her slipper off again.)* Bring it back!

SERVANT. Princess, your father, the Sultan, comes.

(Enter from the left the SULTAN, the VIZIER, and ZOBEIDA. The SERVANTS bow their heads to the ground, the PRINCESS rises and bows slightly. The SULTAN takes his seat upon the divan, the GRAND VIZIER at his right, the PRINCESS and ZOBEIDA stand at his left. The SERVANTS sit lower than the rest of them.)

SULTAN. *(Pompously, as always.)* My daughter, moon of my delight, essence of beauty, I have news for you.

PRINCESS. *(Salaams.)* Yes, oh, Exalted Parent.

SULTAN. You are to marry the son of this worthy woman — this — ah — gazelle of beauty!

(He gestures to ZOBEIDA, who salaams.)

PRINCESS. *(Salaams.)* Your word, Exalted Parent, is my law.

SULTAN. Her son is the Caliph of Chrysophrand.

PRINCESS. Chrysophrand?

ZOBEIDA. Where the chrysophrase comes from.

SULTAN and **VIZIER.** Certainly, where the chrysophrase comes from.

PRINCESS. Oh, yes, certainly — where the chrysophrase comes from.

SULTAN. And he has more treasure than in all the lands of Cathay. Mines full of rubies large as pomegranates — orchards full of cherries big as melons — pearl beds yielding bushels of pearls a month. What else?

Plays for Children

ZOBEIDA. Uncounted herds of elephants, a palace of ivory and porphyry and gold and chrysophrase —

SULTAN. Behold the jewels he has sent me!

(VIZIER holds out bowl of jewels to PRINCESS.)

PRINCESS. Oh, what emeralds! What pearls!

(She holds up a string of jewels in wonder.)

SULTAN. *(Complacently.)* Yes, he will make a fine husband for my daughter.

VIZIER. True, oh Celestial Ruler.

SULTAN. *(To ZOBEIDA.)* Did you say he was coming soon?

ZOBEIDA. Yes, he said he was coming right away.

(She looks nervously at the door. The SERVANT rises and with bowed head says:)

SERVANT. Oh, Celestial Sultan, the people come for favors and for judgment.

SULTAN. We will receive them.

SERVANT. *(Calling.)* Let the people enter for favors and for judgment.

(With noise and tumult a crowd of people enter from the middle aisle through the audience. The MAGICIAN and JULLANAR are among them. The people crowd up on the stage. Two men SERVANTS enter, from right and left entrances, and push the people back into groups at left and right of stage, the VIZIER helping. Two old men break out from groups and run, quarrelling, in front of SULTAN.)

FIRST OLD MAN. Celestial Ruler, he stole my pig.

SECOND OLD MAN. Celestial Ruler — no — no —it was my pig.

FIRST OLD MAN. He lies, he lies! It was my pig.

SECOND OLD MAN. It was my pig!

SERVANT. Cease, cease!

(They try to push the quarrelers back.)

FIRST OLD MAN. *(Shouting.)* It was my pig! Mine — mine — mine!

VIZIER. Back — back — would you deafen the Sultan with your pigs?

SULTAN. *(Rising on steps of divan.)* Silence all! *(There is silence.)* I would meditate a moment, that Justice may steal into my mind and heart, and that my words may bring good to all.

Plays for Children

VIZIER. Silence, while the Sultan meditates.

SERVANT. *(To audience.)* Silence, while the Sultan meditates.

> *(The SULTAN sits with finger-tips touching, eyes closed. He meditates. The crowd is still. The MAGICIAN beckons JULLANAR down to the front and says:)*

MAGICIAN. Aladdin is coming. If you wish to save him from the disaster of marrying the Princess, get that lamp which he wears at his belt. Unless I have that lamp, evil will follow him as a shadow on a day of sunlight. Demons will pursue him unless I have that lamp.

JULLANAR. I will save him. I will get it from him!

> *(The SERVATNS at the right and left look out over audience and call.)*

TWO SERVANTS. Oh, Celestial Sultan, the Caliph of Chrysophrand approaches.

CROWD. The Caliph of Chrysophrand! The Caliph of Chrysophrand!

> *(Through the audience two SERVANTS walk, carrying trays of jewels, fruit, and gifts upon their heads. ALADDIN follows them, walking as a king.)*

SERVANTS. Make way, make way for the Caliph of Chrysophrand! Back there — back there, old man — out of the way, woman!

> *(ALADDIN comes up the steps from the audience and the crowd kneels.)*

CROWD. *(Shouting.)* The Caliph of Chrysophrand!

ALADDIN. Salutations, oh Celestial Sultan! Greetings, oh People!

> *(The SERVANTS lay their trays before the SULTAN.)*

SULTAN. Hail, oh noble ruler of Chrysophrand.

VIZIER. Hail — oh noble ruler.

ALADDIN. And have my gifts found favor in your sight, and may I have the hand of your daughter in marriage?

SULTAN. They have found favor in our sight and you may. *(The GRAND VIZIER pulls his sleeve.)* What?

VIZIER. It would be wise, oh Sultan, to make him prove his power and wealth. If he is, indeed, the Caliph of Chrysophrand, ask him if he can do something difficult — build a tower, or a temple.

PRINCESS. *(Clapping her hands.)* No, no! A palace, a new palace for me — out in your garden, Father.

Plays for Children

SULTAN. Well, yes. *(To ALADDIN.)* Can you do it? Build a palace for my daughter? What sort of a palace, daughter?

PRINCESS. *(Delightedly.)* Oh, a wonderful palace — one of gold and silver and ivory and porphyry — with gardens full of flowers —

ALADDIN. The scent of jasmine flowers in the dusk.

PRINCESS. *(With excitement.)* Oh, you…? *(She claps her hands over her mouth.)*

ALADDIN. I am the Caliph of Chrysophrand. And I shall build you the palace you desire. Servants, draw the golden arras. *(The SERVANTS draw the arras behind the SULTAN.)* Now close your eyes, oh people! *(Everyone closes their eyes, but JULLANAR who dashes out from the crowd and tries to snatch the lamp from ALADDIN'S hands. ALADDIN says in horrified astonishment:)* Jullanar!

JULLANAR. Give it to me! Give it to me! It works you harm!

FIRST OLD MAN. She has attacked the noble Caliph!

CROWD. She has attacked the noble Caliph!

SULTAN. Take the girl and throw her to the tigers.

(They take JULLANAR by one arm.)

ALADDIN. Oh, Celestial Sultan, may I, instead, have the girl as my servant?

SULTAN. Why yes, if you want her.

ALADDIN. *(To SERVANT.)* Aside, please. *(The SERVANT stands aside. The MAGICIAN edges toward her.)* Now, oh Celestial Sultan, and oh Princess, if you wish the palace of ivory and gold, close your eyes. I, the Caliph of Chrysophrand, command it on pain of demons and winged dragons. *(A clash of cymbals is heard.)* Are your eyes closed, oh Sultan, and ye people? *(Turns to audience.)* Are your eyes closed, oh ye people of the market place?

CHOWD. Yes — Yes —

ALADDIN. Let there be built in the Sultan's empty gardens a palace such as the Princess desires. *(There is a second clash of cymbals.)* It is done — draw back the arras!

(They draw back the arras and a gorgeous palace is seen outside in the SULTAN'S gardens. The SULTAN rises and looks in amazement. The crowd gasps.)

CROWD. Ohhh — a palace — a palace — gold — ivory — porphyry — how the pinnacles glitter — jewels!

(The crowd edges toward the window to see it.)

MAGICIAN. *(To JULLANAR while the crowd looks at the palace.)* When you hear me outside his palace gate crying out, "New lamps for old," get me that lamp!

JULLANAR. I will — I will!

(The MAGICIAN goes out.)

VIZIER. *(To CROWD.)* Back, back, the Sultan wishes to speak!

SERVANT. Back there — back!

FIRST OLD MAN. But he stole my pig,

SECOND OLD MAN. It was mine — it was mine —

SERVANT. Silence there — with your pigs!

SULTAN. Never has such a wonder as the building of that palace been performed in all the history of Cathay. He is indeed the Caliph of Chrysophrand. I would announce to all my realms that to him I give my daughter Badroulbadour in marriage — my moon-flower of delight!

(He puts her hand in ALADDIN'S. ZOBEIDA grins in delight. Music swells as the light fade.)

ACT TWO

Scene 2

The Court of Aladdin's Palace.

When the lights rise ALADDIN and BADROTJLBADOUR are reclining on a divan. He is playing a stringed instrument and singing.

ALADDIN. "Her cheek is rose,
   Her lips drop wine;
   Her hair is night and her face — moonshine —"

PRINCESS. *(Yawns.)* Do sing a new song, Aladdin!

ALADDIN. *(Surprised.)* Why, my jasmine flower, I was comparing you to the moon.

PRINCESS. *(Playing with beads about his neck.)* Yes, and I get so tired of being always compared to the moon.

ALADDIN. But it is so beautiful.

PRINCESS. Do not go on your tiger hunt today, Aladdin.

Plays for Children

ALADDIN. But I must, Badroulbadour. The Princes I invited are even now dressing in their hunting robes. I cannot stay at home.

PRINCESS. *(Pouting.)* Oh, very well, but some tiger will eat you up, I know.

ALADDIN. What nonsense!

PRINCESS. Oh, yes it will. I have a feeling of some evil near.

ALADDIN. Oh, foolish one — if you fear evil — guard yourself well, my Princess. You will speak to no man while I am away. And if you ride out in your litter, take twice the number of guards.

PRINCESS. Yes, my lord, nor must I, I suppose, drop any jasmine flowers through the curtains to ragged street boys in the dusk.

ALADDIN. By no means —

(JULLANAR crawls out from around one corner of the divan, and, pulling off a pillow, throws it at ALADDIN. He grabs her by her collar and pulls her up. He stands up and shakes her gently.)

ALADDIN. Jullanar — you imp of mischief!

PRINCESS. *(Not unkindly.)* She should have been thrown to the tigers.

JULLANAR. *(Pulls herself away and dances impishly.)* "A sparrow found a shiny stone and made it in a crown; ' I am a caliph now,' he said — 'a caliph of renown.'"

PRINCESS. I think that's very rude, Jullanar, to call your lord Aladdin a sparrow.

JULLANAR. My lord Aladdin — humph — how many times have we begged in the streets together — my lord Aladdin?

ALADDIN. Too often to be forgotten, Jullanar. When I am gone on my tiger hunt, will you be good? Will you do what the Princess tells you? Will you obey her, Jullanar?

JULLANAR. *(With a spurt of anger.)* I will never obey her.

PRINCESS. *(Yawning.)* She still hates me, don't you, Jullanar?

ALADDIN. What nonsense, no one could hate you! *(He takes the lamp from his sash and hands it to JULLANAR.)* Please put this in the red lacquer chest beside my bed, Jullanar. I am afraid it may be lost while I am hunting.

PRINCESS. Oh, that old tarnished lamp! I wish you wouldn't always carry it about with you. Why do you, Aladdin?

ALADDIN. It is a symbol.

Plays for Children

ZOBEIDA. *(Enters, bustling. She wears beautiful garments.)* Aladdin, Aladdin, don't you know the Princes are waiting for you? Your white stallion is so restless, it takes four servants to hold him.

ALADDIN. Then I must be gone. *(Two SERVANTS enter from the right, each bearing a large basket. ALADDIN speaks to them.)* Have you the gold coins for the populace?

SERVANT. In this basket, oh Caliph.

JULLANAR. *(Snickering.)* A sparrow found a shiny stone —

PRINCESS. Be still —

ALADDIN. But it is true, my Princess. *(He laughs.)* I am that sparrow! *(To SERVANTS.)* Have you the candy and sweet meats for the street children?

SERVANT. In this basket, oh Caliph.

ALADDIN. Good! Farewell, Mother! Farewell, my Princess! Farewell, Jullanar. Your sparrow goes to hunt a tiger. Farewell!

(He goes out, followed by SERVANTS.)

PRINCESS. Aladdin, farewell.

(ZOBEIDA sits on a bench, and does some sewing. The PRINCESS reclines on the divan. JULLANAR tries to look through the latch of the rear gate. Tumult grows outside and she pulls a chair to the gate and looks over the top. She has carelessly dropped the lamp on the divan and the PRINCESS picks it up and looks at it, idly.)

JULLANAR. Oh, there goes Aladdin on his white stallion. Oh, how it rears and dances! It has new gold trappings and red tassels. And there go the elephants. Oh — how many — and the beaters on ponies, and the slaves — oh! *(Tumult subsides gradually.)* There they go among the banyan trees of the wide road — there are too many trees to see them.

PRINCESS. How many days did Aladdin say he would be gone?

ZOBEIDA. For seven nights.

PRINCESS. Seven nights is too many! How tarnished this lamp is. *(She rubs it idly.)* I wish he would be with me tomorrow night. Just as the sun goes down — I wish he would be in this garden with me.

(There is a clash of cymbals.)

ZOBEIDA. What noise was that?

PRINCESS. I don't know. Jullanar, have the hunters passed?

Plays for Children

JULLANAR. Yes, they have gone.

PRINCESS. *(Yawning.)* I wish something different would happen — something new and exciting. Would it not be well for you to take this lamp up to Aladdin's chest? Please do it.

JULLANAR. *(Still looking over gate.)* Hmm — there is someone coining down the roadway.

PRINCESS. Who is it?

JULLANAR. An old man — tall — he carries a heavy load.

ZOBEIDA. A load of what?

JULLANAR. Something that shines and sparkles in the sun.

PBINCESS. *(With excitement.)* Jewels?

JULLANAR. No — too big for jewels. He carries a long pole across his shoulders, with lamps, and lanterns hanging from it — new ones, shiny as new coined gold — a fine tall man.

PRINCESS. Oh, let me see him.

(She gets up and goes toward window.)

MAGICIAN. *(Calls outside.)* New lamps for old — new lamps for old.

JULLANAR. New lamps for old — new lamps for old.

(She turns, excited and frightened. ZOBEIDA pulls her down from chair.)

ZOBEIDA. Let me up there to see.

JULLANAR. No — no.

(ZOBEIDA tries to climb up.)

PRINCESS. You are too old, exalted mother-in-law. Let me—let me!

ZOBEIDA. It is not fitting for you.

JULLANAR. Let me!

MAGICIAN. *(Just outside gate.)* New lamps for old — new lamps for old!

PRINCESS. What can he mean?

(There is a loud knocking at the gate.)

MAGICIAN. *(Outside.)* New lamps for old. *(He chants.)* If anyone has an old lamp — I will give him for it a new — a shining jewelled new lamp — I will give in exchange for an old lamp.

JULLANAR. *(Rushes and gets ALADDIN'S lamp.)* Here is this old lamp for him.

PRINCESS. *(Hesitating.)* But Aladdin values it —

ZOBEIDA. Foolishness, he would be far better pleased with a new one.

PRINCESS. *(Still hesitating.)* But why did he value it?

ZOBEIDA. Oh, he made up some tale about it long before he was the Caliph.

JULLANAR. Aladdin was always making up tales and stories of treasure and dragons and genii.

ZOBEIDA. Yes, this tale was all about treasure and a genie — and I declare I thought I saw the creature, he was so real. But, of course, it was just a lot of nonsense.

MAGICIAN. *(Outside.)* New lamps for old.

JULLANAR. Give him the lamp.

PRINCESS. I do so hate old things. *(Calling out the window.)* Oh, Vendor, wait — wait a minute! Would this lamp do?

MAGICIAN. *(Outside.)* It's old and tarnished.

PRINCESS. I did want a new and jewelled one!

MAGICIAN. *(Outside.)* Well, let me see it.

(She throws down the lamp.)

PRINCESS. Now, a jewelled one in exchange.

MAGICIAN. *(Outside.)* May the gate be opened for me?

(There is a clash of cymbals and smoke, and the gate swings open, showing a background of trees, and green beyond a path. The women rush to right rear of stage terrified. The MAGICIAN strides in the gate holding lamp.)

PRINCESS. *(Terrified.)* Oh — oh — out — away!

ZOBEIDA. *(Rushes up to MAGICIAN.)* Oh — the brother of my husband! What joy to see you again!

MAGICIAN. *(Roughly, pushing her away.)* Woman — away!

PRINCESS. *(Calling.)* Guards — come — come!

(GUARDS pour in at left and right with weapons. They are about to fall upon the MAGICIAN. He rubs the lamp.)

MAGICIAN. May you all be powerless to hurt me!

(The GUARDS stand like statues, with arms upraised. ZOBEIDA and JULLANAR cling together, but the PRINCESS steps forward.)

PRINCESS. Out of my garden — dog!

Plays for Children

MAGICIAN. I am Master here now.

PRINCESS. Aladdin is Master.

MAGICIAN. *(Laughing.)* Ha — ha — ha!

PRINCESS. You cannot frighten me. Aladdin will let no harm come.

MAGICIAN. Aladdin is hunting tigers and you will soon be safely very far away.

PRINCESS. Where, may I ask?

MAGICIAN. Guard, close the gate. *(A frightened GUARD does so. The MAGICIAN holds the lamp high and rubs it.)* Oh, Genie of the Lamp, summon your brother genii of the whirlwind and the storm — of the tempest and the tornado — from the realm of Magic, from the Mountains of Kaf — put your wings beneath the floors of the palace, bear us away, away, and away, away into the middle of Ahricanah. Come!

PRINCESS. *(Bravely.)* Aladdin will save us.

(There is clash of cymbals, rumbling, the light goes out.)

ACT TWO

Scene 3

The street in Cathay.

When the lights rise the stage is empty. Enter from the right, ABDALLA, and from the left, TUNKAH, with their usual odd gait. They meet in the center and bow.

ABDALLA. Greetings, sister Tunkah.

TUNKAH. Greetings, brother Abdalla.

ABDALLA. Is all well with you?

TUNKAH. Oh, very well. The world smiles upon me since Aladdin has been made Caliph of Chrysophrand.

ABDALLA. *(Grudgingly.)* Well, it does not frown on me.

TUNKAH. I have more food and clothes than I can use.

ABDALLA. That is good — that is good.

TUNKAH. Aladdin has been very generous — I never thought he had it in him!

ABDALLA. No, I never thought he had it in him.

(Enter through the audience, VIZIER, and attending SERVATNS.)

Plays for Children

VIZIER. *(Calling out.)* Aladdin — Aladdin — has anyone seen Aladdin, the Caliph of Chrysophrand? Anyone who knows the whereabouts of Aladdin, the Caliph of Chrysophrand, will receive a bag of gold! Anyone who can tell the whereabouts of Aladdin, Caliph of Chrysophrand, will receive an elephant from the Sultan himself. *(He addresses TUNKAH and ABDALLA.)* Have you seen Aladdin, the Caliph of Chrysophrand, since yesterday morn?

TUNKAH. No, we have not seen Aladdin!

VIZIER. They say he has become separated from his hunting party.

ABDALLA. We have not seen Aladdin!

VIZIER. Then I suppose you have not seen the palace of the Princess?

TUNKAH. Where?

VIZIER. *(Vaguely.)* Oh, anywhere about the countryside.

TUNKAH. *(To ABDALLA.)* The man is crazy.

VIZIER. If we cannot find the palace of the Princess, we must find Aladdin. *(To SERVANTS.)* Forward!

(They exit. The OLD MAN runs in.)

OLD MAN. The palace is gone — the Princess is gone — Aladdin is gone! The Sultan is frantic. The servants are hunting all over the country for trace of the palace. If Aladdin is found he will be taken to prison!

TUNKAH. What woe is this — a palace lost like a tailor's thimble?

OLD MAN. Come, see the hole the palace has vanished from.

ABDALLA. And has the Princess gone too?

OLD MAN. The Princess and the palace — gone, like smoke!

ABDALLA and **TUNKAH.** Oh, woe — woe — woe!

(They, and the OLD MAN, trot out left. There is a noise of Children talking and laughing off stage. ALADDIN enters, right, with SERVANT carrying basket, and CHILDREN crowding about him. He, too, is laughing and pretending to push them away.)

ALADDIN. Off — keep off there, small demons!

FIRST CHILD. He didn't forget — he didn't forget us.

SECOND CHILD. What kind of candy and sweetmeats — oh — oh!

ALADDIN. *(Taking small candies out of basket.)* Hold out your hands. I have the best sweetmeat cook in all Cathay. Hold out your hands —

39

Plays for Children

catch — catch! Fill your sashes! Take some home to your brothers and sisters, the little ones. Let me tell you a story.

(TUNKAH and ABDALLA enter.)

TUNKAH. Aladdin — Aladdin — run — fly — fly!

ALADDIN. Fly, dear Tunkah? I am not really a crane or a sparrow. I cannot fly. *(He pretends to fly, flapping his arms.)* Where shall I fly to?

(The CHILDREN laugh as ALADDIN capers about.)

TUNKAH. This is no time for teasing.

ABDALLA. You must go, Aladdin.

ALADDIN. Why should I go?

ABDALLA. *(Looking down the street.)* The Grand Vizier.

TUNKAH. *(Shrieking.)* Run — Aladdin — run!

(They grab his hands to pull him away, but he forms a circle with them and dances about.)

ALADDIN. Dance — dance — lift up your feet — sing — sing — for joy of dreams come true!

(Enter VIZIER, and SERVANTS.)

VIZIER. There is the evil demon! Seize and bind that man!

(The SERVANTS go forward toward ALADDIN, who stands with folded arms, looking at the VIZIER.)

ALADDIN. Dogs, touch not the Caliph of Chrysophrand.

VIZIER. *(Angrily to slaves.)* Why do you not obey me? *(To ALADDIN.)* It is the command of the Sultan that you shall be thrown into the dungeon.

ALADDIN. You need not bind me. I shall not fly, or run. You cannot hurt me, for I am not afraid. That is a charm I have — a magic charm. Run home, children, run quickly. Show me which is the quickest — run! *(The children run out. ALADDIN turns to VIZIER.)* Why, please, does the Sultan demand my imprisonment? What have I done?

VIZIER. You have willfully and evilly, by the arts of the blackest magic, moved and spirited away the palace of Badroulbadour and the Princess herself.

ALADDIN. *(Amazed.)* What?

TUNKAH. We've been trying to tell you. Your palace and the Princess are lost!

ALADDIN. *(Dazed.)* My palace and the Princess — lost?

ABDALLA. Lost — like a tailor's thimble!

ALADDIN. But they cannot be lost. A palace cannot vanish!

VIZIER. It cannot — but it has.

ALADDIN. But not the Princess!

VIZIER. That is why you are to be arrested.

ALADDIN. *(Wildly.)* If my Princess has gone, I have no wish to live. I wish I may go to her and find her.

(There is a clash of cymbals, smoke, darkness. When it clears ALADDIN has gone.)

VIZIER. Where is he? Where is Aladdin? Servants, find Aladdin!

(The SERVANTS rush about the street.)

TUNKAH and **ABDALLA**. *(Taking hold of each other's hands and jig up and down with joy.)* He has escaped! Aladdin is safe! He has vanished!

VIZIER. The Sultan will be frantic. Find Aladdin!

(He and the SERVATNS rush down through the audience, calling, asking the audience:)

SERVATNS. Aladdin — Aladdin — does anyone know the whereabouts of Aladdin?

TUNKAH and **ABDALLA**. Aladdin is safe!

(The lights fade.)

ACT TWO
Scene 4

The Court of Aladdin's Palace now transported to Ahricanah. Everything is the same, except the background has now changed.

ZOBEIDA is sitting upon a stool, sewing; BADROULBADOUR is pacing back and forth, fanning herself; JULLANAR is shaking the locked garden gate, trying to open it.

JULLANAR. I wish I hadn't done it! I wish I hadn't made you give him that lamp.

PRINCESS. I gave it to him myself. We all wish we hadn't.

Plays for Children

JULLANAR. But it was all my fault. I was angry at Aladdin.

ZOBEIDA. Evil always follows in the path of anger.

JULLANAR. I am a beast. I hated you, oh, Princess, and I was angry at Aladdin, and I listened to the evil words of the Magician. I am a beast — a pig — a worm!

PRINCESS. *(Kindly.)* Stop crying, Jullanar. The harm is done.

JULLANAR. I hate this place. It is so hot, so breathless.

PRINCESS. That gate is tightly locked, Jullanar. Look out, and see if anyone is coming across the desert.

(JULLANAR draws a small table to gate and climbs it, looking over.)

ZOBEIDA. Who but a camel could cross that desert?

JULLANAR. I think that someone might cross it. There is a sort of sandy path that leads among the yellow dunes.

PRINCESS. Let us try it. I think we could climb the gate, Jullanar. I must not stay here a captive of the Magician's. I would rather die in the desert.

ZOBEIDA. Humph — you would die, surely.

PRINCESS. But, worthy mother-in-law, I must try to escape. Will you not come with me?

JULLANAR. The Magician will come into the garden at any moment.

ZOBEIDA. Well, let me see if it seems possible. *(She goes over to the taboret. The others push her up on it with difficulty.)* Oh — I'm falling — oh — oh — *(Looking over.)* What a horrid desert.

JULLANAR. Now pull, and put your leg up. Climb now, climb!

PRINCESS. Do you want the Magician to catch you?

JULLANAR. Pull now. It will not hurt you to drop in the sand on the other side.

ZOBEIDA. Oh, I can't — I could never do it — oh — oh — I'm stuck.

PRINCESS. No, you aren't. Push her, Jullanar! *(They push, and ZOBEIDA flops over the gate.)* Now you, Jullanar.

JULLANAR. No, Princess, — for Aladdin's sake — you next.

PRINCESS. Oh, very well. Kick the table over as you climb, so the Magician will not know where we have gone. We will hide among the sand dunes till the night. *(She climbs the gate.)* Hurry, Jullanar, and follow me.

(She drops out of sight. JULLANAR climbs after her, and is perched on top of the gate, when the MAGICIAN enters.)

MAGICIAN. It seems that I have come at an awkward moment.

JULLANAR. I — I was just looking at the desert.

MAGICIAN. Yes, beautiful view, is it not? So broad and extensive! Come down, Jullanar.

JULLANAR. I won't. I hate you. You are a demon — a sorcerer — a serpent!

MAGICIAN. *(Mocking her.)* A ssss-orcerer — a ssss-erpent. Get down, Jullanar.

JULLANAR. I should never have listened to you. I should have known you were not to be trusted. I hate you.

MAGICIAN. Hate is a dangerous weapon, Jullanar. It turns in the hand. Oh, slaves! *(SLAVES run in.)* Go out into the desert, and bring in Zobeida and the Princess. Come down, Jullanar.

(He takes her down. The SLAVES run out of the gate, leaving it open. A wide expanse of desert and some palm trees show. The MAGICIAN shakes JULLANAR as he puts her on the floor.)

JULLANAR. *(Glaring.)* They are not in the desert. They are sleeping in their rooms.

MAGICIAN. It is as bad to lie as to hate, Jullanar. *(He looks out of the gate.)* It is nearly sunset. How beautiful it is across the sands, the colors like gold and silver and opal and amethyst. How foolish for them to think they can walk across the desert, Jullanar. I suppose they thought they might find their way home across the great flat world to Aladdin. *(He chuckles.)* Aladdin is very far away on his tiger hunt. Ah, ha — my slaves are bringing them back. They did not go far. If you are not a very good girl, Jullanar, I will curse you with demons.

(The SLAVES enter with ZOBEIDA and the PRINCESS. The MAGICIAN closes and locks the gate.)

PRINCESS. *(Regally.)* Why did you send them to interfere with me?

MAGICIAN. *(Laughing.)* Because it was my pleasure. You did not have a very long walk, did you? Did you enjoy it?

PRINCESS. Greatly, it was most pleasant.

ZOBEIDA. Oh, woe — woe!

Plays for Children

MAGICIAN. *(To SLAVES, ZOBEIDA, and JULLANAR.)* Away — I would see Badroulbadour alone! *(They exit.)* I like your spirit.

PRINCESS. I do not like yours.

MAGICIAN. But I do not like your manners.

PRINCESS. Nor I yours.

MAGICIAN. I will have no more of such answers.

PRINCESS. I shall speak to you as I wish.

MAGICIAN. You know no fear, do you?

>*(He puts his hand on her forehead, and bends her head back, looking into her eyes.)*

PRINCESS. *(Shaking her head free.)* No, a Princess is never afraid, Aladdin says...

MAGICIAN. Aladdin says — Aladdin this — Aladdin that — always Aladdin! Let me never hear his name again! I am your master now, remember. *(He goes toward door and turns.)* I shall return soon. *(He looks at the sky.)* At sunset. Have the evening meal ready and curb your rebellious spirit. Do you understand?

PRINCESS. Yes.

MAGICIAN. Yes, my lord.

PRINCESS. Yes.

MAGICIAN. Yes, my lord.

PRINCESS. *(Sweetly.)* Yes.

MAGICIAN. *(Shrugs shoulders.)* Oh, very well. We shall see later who is master — you — or I.

>*(He exits. The PRINCESS watches him, then flings herself on the divan.)*

PRINCESS. Oh, Aladdin — Aladdin! Come to me — come!

>*(There is a clash of cymbals and darkness. Then lights. ALADDIN stands, astonished, in the center of the stage. The PRINCESS sits up on the divan, gazing at him. She holds open her arms, and he rushes to her. They embrace.)*

PRINCESS. Aladdin!

ALADDIN. Are you safe? Are you unharmed?

PRINCESS. Yes, yes. But the Magician is terrible!

ALADDIN. Ah, I shall deal with him! Where are we?

PRINCESS. In the middle of Ahricanah. He wished us here with his lamp.

ALADDIN. Where is his lamp?

PRINCESS. On his sash.

ALADDIN. I must get it back.

PRINCESS. But how did you get here?

ALADDIN. I have no idea. I was in the dungeon, and then, in a flash — I am with you in Africa.

PRINCESS. Oh, I know, I know! Yesterday, in the morning, when you left me for the tiger hunt, I wished that you might be with me this evening at sunset, and, as I wished, I rubbed the lamp.

ALADDIN. A lucky wish.

PRINCESS. I always wish you with me, Aladdin. But what shall we do? The Magician will return in a moment.

ALADDIN. Let me think. I shall hide here beneath this divan. When he comes for his evening meal, ply him with foods, and treat him pleasantly. Dance for him, and, when he is not watching, I shall grab the lamp, and wish us all back to Cathay again.

PRINCESS. But if he wishes first — if he should wish that you were dead!

ALADDIN. Think not of evil possibilities.

PRINCESS. Someone is coming — hide — hide!

(ALADDIN crawls under divan. ZOBEIDA, JULLANAR, and SLAVES bearing trays of food, enter, left. The PRINCESS sings.)

PRINCESS. "Scent of ambergris and musk — Jasmine flowers through the dusk—"

ZOBEIDA. *(Reprovingly.)* I thought to find you weeping.

PRINCESS. Why should one weep — no — no — rather dance and sing! *(ZOBEIDA goes to sit on divan.)* No, no, honored mother-in-law, sit not there — that is — not there — see the clouds of the sunset — like boats sailing on a river of dreams — *(She steers her over to a taboret as she talks.)*

ZOBEIDA. What is the matter with you, Badroulbadour? You seem so odd.

PRINCESS. No, no — only my spirits are happier. The Magician will be here in a moment. Jullanar —

JULLANAR. Yes, Princess.

(The MAGICIAN enters, left. The women salaam deeply. JULLANAH, watching closely, sits at one end of the divan. The MAGICIAN sits on a stool in the center of the stage behind a table set with food. The PRINCESS serves him.)

MAGICIAN. Ha, ha — this is better than it was. My words have done some good.

PRINCESS. *(Passing food.)* The words of my lord have wrought a great change within my heart.

MAGICIAN. I am rejoiced to see it. Serve my wine, Badroulbadour,

PRINCESS. With joy.

MAGICIAN. I knew I could tame that rebellious spirit.

PRINCESS. The presence of my lord works miracles.

(She looks involuntarily toward the divan.)

MAGICIAN. *(Watching her fixedly.)* There is something strange about you, Badroulbadour.

PRINCESS. No, no. There is nothing, nothing. I merely decided to be more amiable, more pleasant —

MAGICIAN. Is that all?

PRINCESS. *(Nervously.)* Let me dance for you. You have never seen me dance.

MAGICIAN. Dance then. *(The PRINCESS dances. The MAGICIAN watches her, and notices that she looks often toward the divan. He leaps to his feet, crying out.)* There is something wrong here!

PRINCESS. No, no.

(She grasps his arm as he strides toward the divan. ALADDIN crawls out.)

ZOBEIDA. Aladdin,!

JTJLLANAR. Aladdin!

(She dashes to the MAGICIAN and pulls the lamp from his sash and hands it to ALADDIN. There is a struggle and tumult. The MAGICIAN throttles ALADDIN and, grasping the lamp, shouts out.)

MAGICIAN. I wish Aladdin —

ALADDIN. *(Tearing lamp from him and shouting:)* I wish this Magician into the darkest depths of the realms of magic. Let him never return.

(Darkness, cymbals, light. The MAGICIAN is gone.)

PRINCESS. Oh, Aladdin, he is gone — he is gone!

ALADDIN. Yes, but we are still in Ahricanah. Now, let us go home.

(Clash of cymbals, darkness, and a rumbling noise. When the light is on again, the background has been changed. The palace is back in Cathay.)

PRINCESS. Banyan trees! We are home again.

(There is knocking at the garden gate.)

ALADDIN. *(Rubbing lamp.)* Let the garden gate be opened.

(It swings open. With great tumult and shouting, a crowd rushes in: the SULTAN, the VIZIER, TUNKAH, ABDALLA, and SERVANTS.)

SULTAN. *(Embraces PRINCESS.)* My daughter — my daughter!

TUNKAH and **ABDALLA.** They are home again — they are home again!

ALADDIN. *(Grasping TUNKAH'S and ABDALLA'S hands.)* Take hands, take hands, the Princess is home! Take hands and form a ring!

(The whole crowd takes hands and forms a gigantic ring on the stage.)

CROWD. *(Skipping wildly around in ring.)* Aladdin is home! Come, dance and shout and sing!

(The lights fade as they rejoice.)

End of Play

Plays for Children

Plays for Children

DICK WHITTINGTON

by Lloyd Bradey

Characters

Dick Whittington
Alice, the cat
Tuck, gang member
Planky, gang member
Gaunt, gang member
John, gang member
Alen, gang member
Leader of the gang
Cook
Alice Fitzwarrn
Mr. Fitzwarrn, her father
Captain Mendenhall
Pirate Chief
Pirates
King of the Spice Islands
Queen of the Spice Islands
Rats
Servants

ACT I
Scene 1
A street in 15th Century London

Scene 2
The scullery, a few weeks later

Act II
Scene 1
On board the ship

Scene 2
The tropical palace grounds of the King of the Spice Islands

Scene 3
The street

Scene 4
The scullery

Scene 5
The scullery

ACT I

Scene 1

A street in 15th Century London.

Church bells begin to sound softly, growing louder, and then fading as a voice comes over them, picking up their rhythm.

VOICE. Welcome, Dick Whittington, welcome to London. Welcome, Dick Whittington, thrice Lord Mayor of London.

> *(Church bells and voice fade off into silence. The lights come up, and several GANG MEMBERS sidle on.)*

TUCK. *(A weasely Cockney type.)* Get anything Planky?

PLANKY. *(Another Cockney.)* Hah! The blinkin' gent nearly caught me, too!

GAUNT. *(Opposite of his name; a navvy type.)* Arr! If you blokes would listen to me sometimes, 'stead of him what calls hisself our leader, you'd get some real takings. Like in here. *(Gesturing toward house.)*

TUCK. In there? Rob a house? Nah, that's not fer me! I'll take me chances with our leader!

> *(He walks away from PLANKY and GAUNT, to meet another group of GANG MEMBERS entering opposite. PLANKY sidles up to GAUNT.)*

PLANKY. Ain't you afraid of what the leader might do?

Plays for Children

GAUNT. Nah! E's just a big bag o' wind! You listen to me, Planky, there's lots of gold for the taking right in there! This is the house of Master Fitzwarren, the richest merchant in all o' Lunnon. Work it right, and it'd be ours!

PLANKY. *(Eagerly.)* Tell me how!

> *(GAUNT looks at him, then the pair drift into a secretive conversation to one side. TUCK has engaged the other GANG MEMBERS in conversation)*

TUCK. Well, lads! Any luck fer the day's work?

JOHN. Nah. I ain't never seen such a day for rotten luck.

ALAN. 'E'll be mad at us with no more to show than a stinkin' ha' pence.

PLANKY. Sounds good. I'll ask them. *(He crosses to the opposite group, leaving GAUNT alone on the corner. The group alerts as PLANKY approaches, swings to face him so their backs are to the entrance.)* Lads, Gaunt over there was just tellin' me how we can fatten all our purses and settle with our leader, too…

> *(The LEADER enters in time to hear the last phrase. PLANKY, seeing him, trails his voice off and backs away.)*

LEADER. *(Silkily.)* Settle with our leader, eh? Now, Planky, what did you have in mind?

PLANKY. *(Backing away as the GANG opens up for LEADER.)* Oh, nothing, nothing.

LEADER. *(A menacing advance.)* Now, now, Planky, let's have none o' that. You're not smart enough. Did Gaunt there give you some ideas?

PLANKY. Him? Nah. I got me own…

> *(The GANG LEADER shoves him aside as he stalks across to GAUHT. The latter holds his ground, but obviously is fearful.)*

LEADER. Now, now, Gaunt. You shouldn't be putting ideas into poor old Planky's head. 'E's got room for only one idea at a time. I suppose you were making your old suggestions about robbing houses. *(His dirk flashes into the open.)* This is saying you ain't going to do it as long as I'm leader of this gang! *(LEADER advances steadily on GAUNT, who suddenly breaks and runs.)* Ha! So you'd be leader of this gang, would you! *(Sheathing dirk.)* Not as long as I'm around! Now lads, what've you got fer the day's work?

> *(There is an awkward silence.)*

51

Plays for Children

ALAN. I never see such tough luck! Not so much as a ha'pence.

LEADER. *(Moving toward him.)* You mean you ain't got nothing? *(Looking from one to the other.)* None of you? Hah! And I thought I had the toughest gang in all of Lunnon! Not afraid to snatch a purse. *(He is advancing from one to the other.)* A bunch of lily-livered rats, that's what you are! *(Suddenly, he grabs JOHN, pulls a drawstring purse from beneath his blouse, and flings him to the ground.)* Hah! Holding out? *(Advancing over the prostrate JOHN.)* You know what happens to men of my gang who hold out?

GAUNT. *(Abruptly.)* Lay off! Someone's coming!

(The GANG scatters and hides. The church bells swell up, and the VOICE repeats the "Welcome Dick Whittington" refrain as DICK WHITTINGTON enters. He is ragged, but clean.)

DICK. Church bells again! But this isn't Sunday. I could swear I heard my name, just as if those bells were talking to me. *(He listens intently; the bells fade out.)* They've stopped. *(Looking around.)* I was told I'd see some wondrous things in London, but I never expected church bells would welcome me. *(He listens again, but there is only silence. Then he shrugs and starts out.)* Oh, well, 'tis no stranger than finding myself, a country lad in London. I expect anything can...

(He stops abruptly as PLANKY sidles in to block his way. They stare tautly at each other briefly, then DICK tries to step around. PLANY blocks his way. DICK turns to go out another way but is blocked by ALAN similarly. Finality he is trapped, ringed by GANG MEMBERS. Then the LEADER emerges and swaggers insolently up to DICK.)

LEADER. Going somewhere?

DICK. *(Bravely, but with full knowledge of his peril.)* I might be. 'Tis my business!

LEADER. Maybe we're going to make it our business!

DICK. What do you want, anyway?

LEADER. Oh, I dunno. We might want a lot of things—like money! Lots of you country clucks bring money with you.

DICK. *(Involuntarily betraying the position of his purse with a hand move.)* I—I haven't got any!

LEADER. *(Noting the movement.)* Oh? Now that's too bad! We've had a luckless day and we might be persuaded to let you go iff'n you were to treat us right.

DICK. I—I told you, I haven't got any!

Plays for Children

(He tries to push through the circle, but is hurled back roughly with ad lib remarks.)

LEADER. No money, an' tryin' to leave our select company! *(A menacing advance.)* That just ain't smart. You better find some in that purse you've got hidden or we might have to get rough!

(There is a moment of tense silence as DICK looks at the menacing leader and the gang. Then suddenly he pulls a home-spun drawstring purse from beneath his rags and flings it center.)

DICK. There you are, then!

(The GANG leaps as one man for the purse. DICK seizes the opportunity to flee, but the LEADER sees him.)

LEADER. He's tryin' to get away lads! Get him! *(The GANG flings itself after DICK, who is mobbed and roughed up as he is forced to return to face the LEADER. The LEADER meanwhile, has leisurely picked up the purse.)* Haw! Thought you'd get away. Now, let's see what's in this purse....Nothing! What're you tryin' to do?

DICK. I told you I didn't have any money! I spent my last penny for a roll last night!

LEADER. Any country cluck what comes up to Lunnon has got to have money or he's got to steal!

GAUNT. Maybe he'd have better luck than we did. 'E's so innocent looking!

LEADER. Shut up! I'm doing this. Now, where's your money?

DICK. I told you I don't have any—and I won't steal!

LEADER. All right! But we don't have to believe you. So now we're going to take you all apart and feed you to the rats!

(Desperately, DICK suddenly wrenches free and darts across the stage. The gang chases him, LEADER standing and watching sardonically. A large white cat bounds onstage, unseen by LEADER or GANG. The CAT should be a dancer.)

LEADER. Catch him! Give him what for! *(CAT advances, claws extended, on LEADER, and springs on him, clawing. LEADER shaking himself free.)* Run lads! Run fer your lives! It's one of them wild Lunnon cats!

(Clothing ripped, he leaps over the sprawling GANG and prostrate DICK, and flees out. The GANG, with various ad lib vocalizations, take in the presence of the CAT, who is advancing menacingly, and flees. CAT leaps in front of one, and there is a bit of cat-and-mouse game until he, too, escapes.

Plays for Children

CAT, with a triumphant glance after them returns to DICK, still prostrate and squats beside him.)

CAT. Mrowr? (Meaning: "What's the matter with him?")

(Gently she strokes DICK who shows no sign of life. CAT strokes him a few more times, then, exasperated, shakes him hard.)

DICK. *(Reviving.)* What hit me? *(Sees CAT, slides away frightened, with a little exclamation.)*

CAT. *(Reassuringly.)* Mrowr! (Meaning, "It's all right, I won't hurt you.")

DICK. *(Warily.)* You aren't going to hurt me?

CAT. *(Bounding closer.)* Mrowr! ("No, I like you.")

(DICK involuntarily slides away again, CAT following. CAT gets alongside him, and rubs him in cat fashion.)

DICK. You mean, you like me? *(CAT nods, and rubs harder.)* Well, thank you. I'm glad you came along—but *(looking around)* what happened to that gang? *(CAT leaps to feet and re-enacts, in pantomime, the events with LEADER and GANG, then bounds back to DICK.)* Oh, you mean you chased the gang away? *(CAT nods proudly.)* Well, thank you. *(Rising.)* I don't know what I would have done if you hadn't come along. But I suppose you'll be off someplace.

CAT. Mrowr! Mrowr! ("No, no!") *(Leaps toward DICK, who flinches.)* Mrowr! Mrowr! ("You don't need to be afraid of me.")

DICK. You're not going to attack me, then? Or leave me?

CAT. *(Shaking head.)* Mrowr!

(CAT gestures to DICK expressing her affection for him, ending beside him. He strokes her.)

DICK. Oh, now I see! You like me! *(CAT excitedly agrees.)* But I don't see how you can! I'm just a poor boy from the country. I don't have any money, I don't have any house with a nice warm fire for you to sit beside, and I don't have even a saucer of milk for you. Come to think of it, I don't have any food for myself. And I'm hungry. You know, Cat, I haven't had anything to eat, except a little roll, for nearly three days now.

(CAT leaps to feet, pantomimes hunting a mouse, catching it and serving DICK.)

DICK. *(With some reaction to the idea of eating a mouse.)* Thank you, Cat, but I don't think I could eat a mouse. *(CAT is disappointed.)* I'm sure you'd think a mouse would be delicious, but I'm not that hungry yet. I wonder if they'd give us something to eat in this house.

(CAT nods excitedly and leaps to one side. DICK knocks at the door. There is no answer. He waits a minute, then speaks dejectedly.)

DICK. Not much use knocking there; no one seems to be at home. *(With a sigh.)* Well, what do we do now? *(Looking around.)* I know this much; I've got to get something to eat pretty soon or I'll keel over. Let's go on to the next house. Come on Cat. Say, what is your name? I can't just call you Cat all the time.

CAT. *(Cocking head quizzically.)* Mrowr? ("What are you talking about?")

DICK. Mrowr isn't a name, it's one of the noises you make. Let's see... How about Iphigenia? *(Cat is horror-struck.)* No? Can't say I blame you. Well—how about Hortense? *(The same reaction.)* No? My, but you're hard to please. Oh, I know! Yesterday when I came through Highgate, I saw a girl riding with her father in their carriage. She had long golden hair and she was wearing a bright green dress with some kind of a yellow scarf around her neck. She was as beautiful as an angel. She didn't see me, of course; I was just one of the crowd, but as she passed, I heard her father call her "Alice." Would you like that for a name? *(Cat indicates her pleasure vigorously.)* You do? Fine! Then Alice it is! Now Alice, let's be on our way and see if that next house has a bit of work we can do for our supper.

(DICK starts off, CAT following. They are stopped by the door bursting open. A slatternly Irish COOK, broom in hand, stands there.)

COOK. Sure, now, and was it you poundin' on this door and disturbing me when I'm makin' supper?

DICK. Yes it was, but I hope I didn't disturb you too much.

COOK. Disturbed I was and plenty. And what do you want?

DICK. Please, ma'am, I was just going to ask if you could spare a bit of bread for me and maybe a saucer of milk for my cat here. We haven't had anything to eat since yesterday.

COOK. *(Coming down threatening.)* Another one of them Lunnon beggars, I'll be bound! The city is overrun with 'em, poundin' on doors and stopping honest folk in the streets and snatching purses! If you was an honest lad instead o' one of those dirty beggars you'd work for yer keep 'sted of begging! Clear out now, before I give you what for with this broom.

Plays for Children

DICK. Oh, but we want to work for our supper! I can chop wood, and cat here can catch rats and mice like you've never seen. Why, she'd soon rid the house of all such vermin!

(CAT starts to pantomime a rat hunt as before, but is interrupted by a threatening gesture and movement of the COOK.)

COOK. Aarrgh! I've heard that before, I have! It's the likes of you who'd rob the household blind! And if I let you in the scullery, the first thing you'd do would be to steal the silver! Now clear out!

(She chases them with broom swinging wildly, but is forced to halt by shortness of breath.)

DICK. No, honest I wouldn't! All I want is a little supper and a corner to sleep in, I'd chop wood and my cat would catch all the rats in your house!

COOK. I'll have you know that there's not a rat or a mouse in my house, it's that clean! *(Advancing on them.)* An' any dirty Lunnon beggar boy who says different had better watch out! Now be off with you!

(She starts to chase DICK and CAT out. ALICE appears in doorway, dressed as Dick had described her. When the chase stops and DICK has an opportunity, he recognizes her as the girl from Highgate.)

ALICE. *(Imperiously.)* Cook, what are you doing?

COCK. *(Startled.)* What? Oh, it's you, Lady Alice. Why, I was just chasin' away two beggars who are tryin' to git into the house to steal the silver!

DICK. *(Indignant.)* We are not!

ALICE. How do you know they'll steal the silver?

COOK. Just look at 'em, yer ladyship. All ragged and dirty! As fine a pair of Lunnon beggars as I've ever seen, and you know what blaggards the Lunnon beggars are. As soon cut a body's throat as look at him.'

DICK. We are not London beggars! *(To ALICE.)* We wouldn't steal the silver, your Ladyship; that isn't honest. All we asked for was crust of bread for me and a drop or two of milk for my cat. I'd chop wood or clean the scullery or do anything that's honest.

ALICE. Is that your cat? My, what a pretty one. She must be an awfully good cat to keep herself that clean.

DICK. She saved my life, too. She's a fine cat, and the only thing I've got. *(Shyly.)* Her name's the same as yours.

ALICE. Alice?

DICK. Uh-huh.

COOK. A fine thing it is to have a dirty old cat named for you. *(CAT leaps at her.)* Aargh! Git the dirty beast away from me!

>*(CAT chases COOK. DICK and ALICE try to catch CAT, shouting their lines as they go.)*

DICK. Alice, stop it!

ALICE. But I'm only trying to help!

DICK. I don't mean you; I mean the cat!

COOK. Help! Help! Get the dirty beast away from me!

>*(DICK and ALICE finally catch CAT, who has been vocalizing throughout, and hold her.)*

DICK. Alice, you naughty cat! You mustn't do things like that!

ALICE. Oh, please don't punish her! After all, Cook did call her a dirty beast.

COOK. Aye, and I'll call her that again! *(CAT hisses and lunges; COOK draws back.)* Lady Alice, be careful. Them two is out to cozen you.

DICK. If you say that again, I'll let Cat go!

ALICE. And you'd be right, too. You know, I think I've seen you before somewhere.

COOK. Beggin' on the streets.

>*(CAT lunges; DICK pulls her back.)*

DICK. Stop it! *(To Alice.)* I don't think you've seen me, but I have seen you.

ALICE. Oh? Where?

DICK. *(Shyly.)* Yesterday at Highgate. I was just coming into London when you drove past in your carriage. You were wearing a dress just like that one. I thought you were the prettiest girl I'd ever seen.

ALICE. Oh that's nice. But I'm sure I saw you there, too. I remember telling Father…

COOK. *(Interrupting.)* He's a real crafty one, he is! He spotted you right away, Lady Alice, and followed you here just so he could steal the silver. Probably this cat led him here!

>*(CAT again lunges, but is restrained.)*

ALICE. Oh, do be quiet, Cook! *(To DICK.)* If I do let you come in and give you some food, will you promise not to steal anything?

Plays for Children

DICK. *(Indignantly.)* I wouldn't steal anything. Not from you or anybody else—but especially not from you.

COOK. Hah! A pretty story he tells when everyone is listening, but I'm thinkin' it'll be a different story when the night is down!

FITZWARREN. *(Entering from off, briskly.)* What would be a different story?

ALICE. *(Running to him.)* Oh, Father, I'm glad you are home. Cook is being mean again.

COOK. 'Tis being mean I am when I'm just trying to protect the family silver from a couple of thievin' Lunnon beggars!

FITZWARREN. London beggars! Cook is right, my dear. The London beggars are very dangerous and they'd as soon cut your throat as look at you. If you have any reason to think a gang of them is around, you must...

DICK. But we're not beggars, sir!

FITZWARREN. Not beggars? Why bless my soul! It's a boy and a cat!

DICK. That's right, sir. 'Tis true we knocked on your door and asked for some food. But I tried to explain both my cat and I would work for it. I'd do anything, chop wood, clean the scullery, anything, and my cat here would catch mice and rats.

FITZWARREN. *(Inspecting the pair.)* This *is* unusual. A beggar lad willing to work for his supper. What is your name, lad?

DICK. Dick Whittington, sir. I'm the third son of a Gloucestershire yeoman and—well, there just wasn't anything for me at home, so I came to London just yesterday looking for a chance to make my fortune—but so far I haven't been able to make enough even for food.

FITZWARREN. Would not your parents care for you?

DICK. They're both dead, sir. I'm an orphan. I've been living with an uncle, but he is poor, and I was too great a burden.

ALICE. He looks honest, Father, even though he's awful ragged. And the cat did save his life.

FITZWARREN. The cat did? How?

DICK. Oh, there isn't much... *(CAT paws at him, indicating she wants to tell the story.)* What? Oh, you want to tell it? All right. I was here, right in the middle of a gang of beggars—and they're all you say they are— and they had knocked me to the ground, like this—go ahead, Alice.

Plays for Children

(*CAT re-enacts the gang fight with considerable gesturing and pride ending with DICK on the ground. He starts to get up, but betraying weakness.*) That was how it was, sir. This gang of beggars would have done me in if Alice—if Alice—

(*DICK sags into faint. General consternation.*)

ALICE. He's fainted! Somebody do something! (*Runs over and kneels beside him.*)

FITZWARREN. What's the matter with him? Get some cold cloths!

COOK. 'Tis my belief he's been struck down with the plague and he'd bring it into the whole household! Saints preserve us!

(*CAT silences COOK with a snarling leap at her. She reels back, terrorized, and CAT returns and stands over DICK pantomiming hunger.*)

ALICE. You mean he's that hungry that he fainted? (*CAT nods.*) Oh, Father, we must help him!

FIZWARREN. We'll not let him starve! (*Helping DICK to feet.*) Come, lad! We'll get you warm by the fire, and then we'll see if there isn't some work you can do after you've eaten. (*To CAT.*) And there'll be a saucer of milk and a place by the fire for you, too.

(*Exits with DICK and ALICE into house. CAT pauses at top step, puts tongue out at COOK, flirts tail, and disappears into house.*)

COOK. Aargh! 'Tis insultin' me you are! But just wait! I'll fix you and your scummy master, too! (*Starts up steps. As she does so church bells begin to sound in rising crescendo. She stops and turns, wonderingly.*) The bells of St. Mary-le-Bow! Now what would they be ringing for at this hour? (*Pause.*) Ah, well, them priest-folk are always ringin' for something!

(*She exits into house. The lights begin to fade, and in the darkness, the voice comes over the bells.*)

VOICE. Welcome, Dick Whittington, Welcome to London. Welcome, Dick Whittington, Come to seek your fortune!

(*Church bells crescendo and segue into in scene-changing cover music as the lights fade to black.*)

ACT I

Scene 2

The scullery, a few weeks later. A fireplace, wood box, table stools, pots and pans.

COOK enters with potatoes, crosses to table and begins working, singing tunelessly.

Plays for Children

COOK. *(Stopping and looking around.)* Now where is that good for nothing Dick? It shouldn't take this long to get wood. I trust him no more today than I did the day he first showed his face, and bad luck that was! And me never knowing when he's going to get his gang to rob the house. *(Grumpily she resumes her work, back to DICK who enters with wood and dumps it in woodbox. Screams.)* Mercy on us all! 'Tis all our throats he'll be slitting!

DICK. What? Who's going to slit whose throat?

(Grabs a knife from the table. COOK reacts, thinking he is after her, and runs away, DICK after her.)

COOK. *(Loudly.)* Heaven help us! 'Tis after me with a knife he is!

DICK. Where are the villains? Don't be afraid, Cook, I'll protect you!

COOK. A fine protector you'd be, trying to slit my throat!

DICK. I slit your throat? *(Realizes the situation, throws knife on table.)* I wouldn't harm you or anyone else. I thought you screamed cause you had seen some robbers.

COOK. *(Waddling over.)* Humph! *(Peering out door.)* Where's your gang? Just waitin' fer your signal, I'll be bound!

DICK. How many times must I tell you I do not have a gang? I don't know why you won't believe it, but I know no one in London save yourself, Lady Alice, and Mr. Fitzwarren. They've been wonderfully kind these weeks, and I hope some day I can repay them.

COOK. I suppose I ain't been kind? Here I work my fingers to the bone fer this family 'specially since Lady Alice' mother died, and what do they do? Saddle me with an orphan beggar boy who ain't got sense enough to wash dishes right! *(Picking up cleaver.)* I ought to fix you good with this! Now get the swab and clean up around the fireplace.

DICK. But, Cook, I did that just before I got the wood! I emptied all the slop jars like you said, took out the garbage, swept the scullery, scrubbed the back steps and cleaned the fireplace and...

COOK. Don't talk back to me, you impertinent spalpeen! And out of the charity o' me heart I fed you when you was half-dead! I'll show you!

(COOK takes after DICK with the cleaver. At the height of the chase, CAT bounds in, COOK nearly collides with her. She backs away from the menacing CAT.)

COOK. There, there! Nice kitty! Dick and I were just havin' a little fun.

Plays for Children

CAT. *(Following, menacing.)* Meowr! ("I don't like you and I don't trust you.")

COOK. *(At Dick's side, stroking him.)* There, see, I love this lad! I love him like I would my own brother!

CAT. Mrowr! ("All right, but I'll keep my eye on you!")

(COOK nervously returns to her potatoes, with side glances toward CAT.)

ALICE. *(Bursting into room.)* Cook, Cook! Come quick!

COOK. What is it, Lady Alice, What is it? Lord save us!

ALICE. Captain Mendenhall is coming.

COOK. Oh, the captain of your father's ship. Sure now, and. is Mr. Fitzwarren goin' to send out a new trading venture to the Spice Islands?

ALICE I guess so, and isn't it wonderful! The captain always brings such beautiful presents—silks and laces and sometimes even jewels. Oh, hello, Dick, I didn't see you there. Oh, and Cook, Father wants to see you so he can tell you what Captain Mendenhall would like for dinner.

COOK. *(Wiping hands on apron.)* Humph! I know what that old sea dog will want. First, there'll be a glass of wine, port or Madeira, followed by a clear soup. Then he'll be askin' me, "Please, Cook, would you be so kind as to give me another glass of wine." Then he'll say, "I hope your roast beef is nice and rare today," and I'll put a piece in front of him so rare that you'd think it might still beller...

(She is out. DICK has kept mopping diligently throughout. ALICE has paid little attention to the COOK, centering her attention on DICK. CAT watches, and pantomimes their growing interest in each other.)

ALICE. Hello, Dick.

DICK. Hello, Lady Alice.

ALICE. It's a nice day, isn't it?

DICK. I guess it is.

ALICE. Wouldn't you like to know what I know?

DICK. How do I know whether I'd like to know what you know until I know what you know?

ALICE. Well, you could guess, couldn't you?

DICK. Yes, if I wanted to.

Plays for Children

ALICE. Don't you want to?

DICK. Want to what?

ALICE. Guess.

DICK. Nope! I'm busy. If I don't get this mopping done, Cook will beat me.

ALICE. Is that all you do—work?

DICK. Yep.

ALICE. And you don't want to guess?

DICK. How do I know if I want to guess until I know what I'm guessing?

ALICE. *(Changing tactics.)* Oh, all right. I'll go talk with Alice. *(With a flirt of her skirt, she crosses to CAT, sits besides her and strokes her. CAT beams.)* Oh, you're such a pretty cat, with nice soft fur. And you're never rude and won't talk.

DICK. I will so talk. I've been talking with you.'

ALICE. *(Ignoring.)* Won't talk to people when they speak to you. Won't even guess when they're asked. I think that's very rude, don't you, Alice?

CAT. *(Beaming.)* Mrowr. ("Absolutely! And let's have some fun with the lad.")

DICK. Oh, Alice, can't you see she's teasing?

ALICE. And besides that, they don't even listen when you've got something important to tell them!

DICK. You never said you had something important! You just wanted me to guess.

ALICE. Then, Alice, they pretend they're too busy! Well, we know what to do then, don't we, Alice?

CAT. Mrowr! ("We certainly do.")

DICK. *(Running to CAT.)* Oh, Alice, that just isn't so! I was busy. If I don't get this mopping done, you know what Cook will do, don't you Alice?

CAT. Mrowr! Mrowr! ("I certainly do.")

DICK. She's already been after me once with that cleaver.

ALICE. She has? Really?

CAT. Mrowr !

ALICE. She did that? Oh, Dick, I'm sorry I teased you. But Cook isn't really that mean to you.

DICK. I don't know how you know that.

CAT. Mrowr. ("Neither do I.")

ALICE. Well, she's always treated me nicely.

DICK. Of course. You're the master's daughter. She wouldn't dare not to.

ALICE. Well, never mind her, Dick. Someday she'll have to look up to you and take orders from you instead of giving them to you.

DICK. Yes, and on that day, cows will fly, too!

ALICE. And today they might start taking flying lessons! Captain…

(She is interrupted by COOK screaming, off.)

COOK. Help! Help! A rat!

(She runs on, whirls about the room. A small rat is pursuing her. DICK grabs his mop and starts swinging at it. CAT stalks the RAT who makes a rush for the door.)

ALICE. *(Peeking through her fingers.)* Is it gone?

DICK. He's gone. Alice will get him, too, I'll bet.

ALICE. Oh, Dick, you were so brave!

DICK. I didn't do anything, Lady Alice. It was Alice who chased the rat. She's a mighty brave cat.

ALICE. She certainly is. Where did that rat come from? I thought we didn't have rats in this house.

COOK. And we never did till he come! *(Jerking thumb toward DICK.)* I was walking past his room on me way back from seein' yer father, an' as I passed his door I heard a sort of scratchin' noise behind me. I stopped an' looked. It's dark in that there hallway an' at first I didn't see nothing. Then, real low down, near the floor, I saw this pair o' beady eyes. Whatever it was it kept creepin' closer an' closer so I started to run in here to get some sort o' weapon, but it kept comin' closer and closer and…

ALICE. Was that when you screamed?

COOK. Scream? I never screamed!

DICK. Somebody screamed, and it sounded just like you.

COOK. People only scream when they're afraid and I'm never afraid.

ALICE. *(Suppressing a giggle.)* Oh!

Plays for Children

COOK. Well, I wasn't. I might have told the rat to go away a bit loudly, but that was all. Then I came in here to git a weapon.

DICK. That was when Alice chased the rat away.

COOK. Alice didn't chase the rat.

DICK. Why, she did so! I saw her with my own eyes. And so did you!

COOK. Then how's it come that she's still here?

DICK. Where?

COOK. *(Pointing to ALICE.)* Right there.

DICK. But that's not Alice—uh—I mean that's not Alice, the Cat, that's the Lady Alice!

ALICE. Well, anyway, she's a very brave cat. *(CAT bounds in picking her teeth.)* Here she is now! Did you catch that old rat?

(CAT nods matter of factly.)

DICK. Did it put up much of a fight?

CAT. Mrowr. ("The tougher they are the better I like it.")

ALICE. How did you catch it?

(CAT pantomimes the chase, ending with eating the rat.)

ALICE. You—you killed it—and ate it?

DICK. Alice you're the best cat there ever was. I wouldn't part with you for all money in London.

COOK. Aarrgh! Making such a fuss over an animal when she's only doing what she's supposed to. *(CAT leaps toward COOK.)* There, there! I was only foolin'. Nice kitty! Brave kitty!

ALICE. Well, are you going to?

DICK. Am I going to what?

ALICE. You remember before all the excitement that I said Captain Mendenhall is coming? *(DICK nods.)* Well, he's the captain of my father's ship, the "Bonaventure." The reason he's coming here is that Father has decided to give every person in the household a chance to send a venture along with him. Isn't that wonderful?

(CAT perks up and listens intently.)

DICK. I guess it would be—if I knew what a venture was.

ALICE. Silly. Everybody knows what a venture is *(But DICK and CAT obviously don't.)* Well, everybody gives the Captain something to trade with—a bolt of cloth, bells, things like that. When he reaches the Spice Islands he trades all these things for gold and silver and diamonds. Then he brings those back and each person gets exactly what he traded.

DICK. Sounds very nice—for someone who's got something to send.

ALICE. Oh, don't be so silly. Everybody's got something to send.

DICK. Well, I haven't!

(CAT, unseen by DICK, leaps to her feet and points to herself.)

ALICE. Oh, you must have! Why, that's the way people get rich! They send out ventures with Captain Mendenhall and he trades and brings back what he got. Then they do it all over again and pretty soon you're rich. That's the way Father did it, and I guess he's one of the richest merchants in all London.

DICK. That sounds fine. But first you've got to earn something to send off, and I haven't had time to do that yet.

COOK. *(Waddling back in with bowl of flour.)* Ay, and if you work like you have so far, you'll never have anything to send off!

ALICE. That's not so! Father says he's one of the hardest working scullery lads we've ever had.

COOK. *(A snort.)* Aaah.'

ALICE. Well, what about it, Dick, are you going to send a venture?

DICK. But Lady Alice, I tell you I haven't got anything.

ALICE. Oh, don't be so stubborn! It's for your own good.

DICK. I ought to know what I've got or haven't got. After all, I'm the one who's got it or hasn't got it.

ALICE. You make me so mad! I'm going to speak to Father.

(Whirls to go out and runs into her FITZWARREN as he enters.)

ALICE. Oh, Father, did I hurt you?

FITZWARREN. No, no, not a bit, but you really should blow a trumpet to warn people when you come through doorways! *(To COOK.)* Captain Mendenhall is here to pick up the ventures of the household. Have you something you wish to send?

COOK. Aye, that I do. I'll be getting it. *(Exits.)*

ALICE. I've been trying to persuade Dick to venture something.

FITZWARREN. And most welcome he would be if he so wishes.

Plays for Children

ALICE. But he's so stubborn! He says he has nothing to send!

DICK. I can't seem to make Lady Alice believe me, sir. 'Tis but the truth I speak.

FITZWARREN. I've never known you not to speak the truth in my hearing, lad. Alice, why will you not believe him?

ALICE. Just because—well—everybody's got something.

FITZWARREN. Alice, lass, listen to me. Dick might very well be telling the truth, first because he'd have no reason to lie, and second because he very well might not have anything to send. Remember how ragged and hungry he was when he first came with us? And finally, well you say everybody's got something, but believe me Alice, everybody doesn't. There are many poor people in this London of ours, people so poor that they'd kill for a slice of bread.

ALICE. I—I guess you're right, Father. *(Brightening.)* Then why don't you give him something to venture?

FITZWARREN. *(Laughing.)* No, lass, 'twould not work. A person's got to make his own venture with something that is his own, something he treasures and would not want to part with. Otherwise, a venture cannot do its work.

ALICE. Well, then, Dick can send Alice.

FITZWARREN. Oh, no, lass. Even if you were his, I could not let…

ALICE. Oh, not me, Alice Fitzwarren. Alice the Cat.

(*CAT reacts with glee.*)

DICK. I could not part with Alice. Why, she's the only thing I've got!

MENDENHALL. *(Entering.)* Mr. Fitzwarren, I cannot tarry much longer. The tide will be turning soon, and I must sail with it.

FITZWARREN. You're quite right, Captain. We're just waiting for Cook's venture—and for Dick here to make up his mind.

DICK. I can't part with Alice. She saved my life!

MENDENHALL. You'll have to be making up your mind, lad. The tide waits for no man.

ALICE. *(To CAT.)* Alice, do you want to help your master make his fortune? *(CAT reacts affirmatively.)* Well then, do you want to go with Captain Mendenhall?

(*CAT goes to DICK'S side, touches him gently as much as to say "This is for your own good," then goes to CAPTAIN'S side.*)

FITZWARREN. Well, lad, it looks as if the cat is more willing than you!

DICK. But Mr. Fitzwarren, she's the only thing I've got!

FITZWARREN. Aye, lad, and you're the only thing she's got. But Captain Mendenhall will see that she gets a good home—and mayhap help make your fortune.

MENDENHALL. Aye, that I will, and who knows what that fortune will be. I know just the place for her, a place where you'll get more good fortune from the trading of this cat than you would from a bushel of diamonds!

ALICE. Oh, that would be nice! And once Dick gets a start, who knows where he might end up! He might even be knighted.

DICK. Oh, that's hardly likely.

FITZWARREN. How about it lad?

DICK. *(Slowly.)* I—I guess it's all right.

FITZWARREN. 'Tis a chance you're taking, but anything worth having is worth taking a chance for. So the matter is settled. Now, Captain, keep a sharp lookout as you near the Spice Islands. There are many reports of pirates in those waters, and I wouldn't want to see you walking a plank.

(MENDENHALL and FITZWARREN exit.)

CAT. Mrowr? ("Aren't you going to say goodbye?")

(Standing in the doorway she makes a small gesture of farewell. DICK can't bear to look, and turns away. CAT leaves slowly.)

DICK. *(Heartbroken.)* Oh, Lady Alice, she was the only creature that ever loved me.

ALICE. She loved you enough to want to help. And I'm still your friend. I'll always be your friend.

DICK. But you're not Alice.

ALICE. I am too Alice, even if I'm not a cat. Come on, let's see them leave!

(She drags DICK off. As they go, COOK, dashes across the stage lugging a trunk as large as she can carry.)

COOK. Hey, now! I got a little somethin' to send, too!

(She is out. The stage is empty, then the bells come up softly and the VOICE comes through them.)

Plays for Children

VOICE. Well done, Dick Whittington, well done!

(The bells crescendo as the lights dim.)

ACT II
Scene 1

On board the ship.

Down the aisle and onto the stage, MENDENHALL and PIRATES in sword play.

PIRATE CHIEF. Come on, ye lily livered swabs! D'you want to live forever. This ship is carrying buckets of gold for the taking!

MENDENHALL. You'll take it over my dead body, you bloody scum of the seven seas! Take that, instead!

1ST SEAMAN. Ho, he sails right into our trap and then thinks he's gonna get away! *(Cut and parry.)*

MENDENHALL. I'm sailing straight for the Spice Islands! The King's fleet will take care of you with a hanging from the yardarm. *(Cut and parry.)*

PIRATE CHIEF. Haw, haw! The King of the Spice Islands! That jelly boned hunk o' lobscouse! He spends all his time eating and none on the care of his ships.

2ND SEAMAN. His ships are so rotten one good sneeze would finish 'em off!

3RD SEAMAN. Let's finish this bloody blighter off right now!

MENDEWEALL. Take that—and that, you yellow-bellied wharf rats!

(FIRST SEAMAN flees.)

PIRATE CHIEF. Come back and fight like a man, you bilge rat! Are you yellow?

1ST SEAMAN. Just sort of orange color! I want to live!

MENDENHALL. Hah, Captain! Your men are like you—run when they face a keen blade! Would you care to try it with me?

PIRATE CHIEF. I hope your will is made because I'm going to carve you up in little pieces and throw you to the rats in the castle of the King of the Spice Islands!

MENDENHALL. Brave words from a yellow-backed sea slug! Have at you!

(Sword play by CAPTAIN and PIRATE CHIEF. Pirates, form semi-circle. CAT enters, behind, takes in situation, stalks up on a seaman, drags him off. This is repeated until one cries out, distracting the PIRATE CHIEF, who is immediately disarmed.)

MENEENHALL. Thank you, Alice. Now both Dick and I are in your debt for our lives. *(To PIRATE CHIEF.)* Come on, you thieving son of an octopus, 'twill be a great pleasure to see you hung!

(Exits, herding PIRATE CHIEF ahead. CAT flicks her tail at audience and follows.)

ACT II
Scene 2

The tropical palace grounds of the King of the Spice Islands.

The KING and QUEEN enter languorously. They speak in carefully modulated tones, being very, very royal, indeed.

KING. My dear, I can't understand what is keeping Captain Mendenhall. I had certain words from the harbormaster that his ship has anchored.

QUEEN. Perhaps he was delayed in town. There are a great many taverns there, you know. *(A large RAT dances across the stage, snatches a bit of food from the table and exits.)* My dear, I do wish you would do something about these rats that infest the castle. Nothing is safe with them around. We can't keep a bit of food in the house.

KING. But what can I do? We have no traps strong enough to hold them, and I don't know anything else that will work.

QUEEN. Poison.

KING. I know, but we lose so many servants that way.

QUEEN. Then put the poison where the servants can't get at it.

KING. There's no place in the castle where they can't get at it.

QUEEN. Then mark the bottles in big letters, P-O-I-S-O-N.

KING. They can't read.

QUEEN. Oh, dear! And good servants are hard to get, too, but there are one or two I wouldn't mind losing. *(SERVANT enters, trips, falls, spilling tray.)* There's one of them now. All right, pick up the mess, and we'll dock your pay. *(SERVANT does so, and scurries out.)* You see what I mean, my dear?

Plays for Children

KING. I do, indeed. And people think that being King and Queen is royal fun. If they only knew!

QUEEN. Oh, there's another one'

> *(SECOND RAT dances through, followed by BABY RAT. SECOND RAT teaches BABY RAT how to steal food from the table, and then the two exit.)*

KING. You know my dear, if we wait much longer for Captain Mendenball, the rats won't leave us anything to eat.

QUEEN. Then let's not wait. The Captain can have the leftovers.

KING. But I thought the dog got those. You know the dog always, gets the leftovers—if the rats leave food to be left over.

QUEEN. Probably that's why the dog has such a lean and hungry look. There's another one! Shoo! Shoo! Shol

> *(THIRD RAT dances on with an impudent gesture, snatches food from table and exits.)*

KING. Perhaps, my dear, Captain Mendenhall will suggest something to deal with these infernal rats. They make me go mad I could swear!

QUEEN. Feel perfectly free. I know exactly how you feel.

KING. You're sure you won't mind?

QUEEN. Of course not. Go right ahead.

KING. Thank you, my dear. Brace yourself. *(QUEEN braces self, shuts eyes, holds hands to ear. King positioning self determinedly, stamps foot.)* My goodness gracious, these rats are sebaceous!

QUEEN. There, now! I hope you feel better.

KING. You have no idea how relieved I feel.

> *(BABY RAT dances back on, followed by SECOND RAT, steals food. SECOND RAT beams maternally, and they are out.)*

QUEEN. You know, I think you were right, I don't think we'll have anything left if we wait for the Captain. Shall we begin?

KING. I quite agree. *(They seat themselves and reach for food. Two RATS snatch it away and exit.)* Why those impertinent, thieving, dastardly—and after I swore at them, too!

SERVANT. *(Entering.)* His Excellency, Captain Mendenhall.

> *(MENDENHALL enters.)*

Plays for Children

KING. My dear Mendenhall! You have no idea how glad we are to see you!

MENDENHALL. And you have no idea, your majesties, how glad I am to be here. I had a brush with pirates just off the Islands, and it looked for a time as though I might not get here at all.

KING. My dear husband, I have told you time and time again that you must do something about those pirates. They might hurt someone!

KING. I intend to, my dear, as soon as I can get the navy off the bottom.

MENDENHALL. Off the bottom, your majesty?

KING. Yes. Would you believe it, Captain, just the other day one of the sailors leaped from the railing to the deck, went right through the main deck, the second deck, the third deck, the fourth deck, the bottom of the ship, and went all the way to the bottom. Naturally, the navy sank.

MENDENHALL. The whole navy, your majesty?

KING. Naturally. Doesn't a ship usually sink when part of it does?

MENDENHALL. Normally, your majesty.

QUEEN. Captain, I trust your voyage has been successful and you have brought some of the latest London fashions for me.

MENDENHALL. Oh, yes, your majesty. I have some especially fine dresses with the new farthingales.

KING. You must tell us about them at dinner, Captain—if we get any. Sit there, Captain.

> *(MENDENHALL sits with KING and QUEEN on either sides of him. KING hands MENDENHALL a dish.)*

KING. Some fried grasshoppers, Captain?

MENDENHALL. Well, I—I—*(A RAT dances in, snatches dish from him and is out.)* What was that?

KING. What was what?

MENDENHALL. That animal.

QUEEN. Just a rat.

KING. We keep a few to amuse the servants. *(SERVANTS run across the stage, chased by all RATS.)* You see? Keeps them from getting fat. Have some octopus steak?

KING. Word for word, and believe me, Captain, she has many words!

71

Plays for Children

MENDENAHLL. Have you tried poison?

KING. Yes, but I can't afford the funerals.

MENDENHAL. Your majesty, it's not necessary to have a funeral for a rat.

KING. Oh, it's not the rats. It's the servants. They can't read the labels.

MENDENHALL. Why don't you teach them how to read?

QUEEN. If they learned to read, they'd know as much as we do, and would quit their positions!

KING. We can't have that!

MENDENHALL. If your majesties will permit me, I may be able to help with your rats.

QUEEN. The rats don't seem to need any help.

KING. Yes, they do well enough without help. I'd hate to see what they'd do with help.

MENDENHALL. No, no your majesties. I had something else in mind—something that may help you get rid of those rats.

KING. *(Bouncing up.)* I'd pay any price and I might even knight the man who rids the castle of these pests!

QUEEN. You should pay even more than that!

MENDENHALL. I have with me as a venture from a smart young lad in London, one of the most powerful rat killers known. Why, this rat killer can kill even a London rat, the most ferocious of all. Rats run at the mere smell of this wonderful agent!

KING. *(Eagerly.)* Tell us more, Captain.

MENDENHALL. I have no more to tell.

KING and **QUEEN.** *(Disappointed.)* Oh!

MENDENHALL. Except that I have such a rat killer with me.

KING and **QUEEN.** Ah!

MENDENHALL. In fact, I believe this rat killer followed me from the ship and is now waiting outside.

KING. Don't stand on ceremony, man! Bring it into our presence.

MEHDENHALL. *(Calling.)* Alice! Alice!

(CAT bounds in gracefully. KING and QUEEN move together, fearfully. CAT moves to CAPTAIN, who strokes her.)

Plays for Children

QUEEN. Oh! What is it?

KING. Animal? Beast? What is it, Captain Mendenhall?

MENDENHALL. Have your majesties never seen a cat?

QUEEN. A cat?

MENDENHALL. Aye. She likes nothing better than to hunt and catch rats. *(With a speculative glance at the KING.)* And believe me, your majesty, when she catches a rat, that rat stays caught!

KING. We shall have to test her abilities, of course.

MENDENHALL. Alice, there are rats here.

(CAT alerts and prowls the stage, hunting.)

KING. There aren't any right at the moment, but if we resume dinner, they'll be right here. Come.

MENDENHALL. Alice, hide and wait. *(All sit, CAT hiding near the CAPTAIN.)* As I was saying, your majesty, Alice is a trading venture…

QUEEN. Shh! Here they are now!

(RATS enter, dancing. They steal food, thumb noses and generally take over the stage. CAT, at the height of this, bounds out. RATS scatter, try to surround CAT and try to attack. Action builds. At one point it seems as though the RATS might win, but CAT finally chases them all out.)

KING. I must have that—that—what did you say it was, Captain?

MENDEHHALL. A cat.

KING. I must have her, I must! I have never seen anything like it in my life!

QUEEN. She was magnificent! We must have her!

MENDENHALL. Well, Alice has shown she can do the work for you.

QUEEN. Alice?

MENDENHALL. The cat's name, your majesty.

QUEEN. Why, Alice is my name, too! 'Tis an auspicious omen. I, as Queen Alice will take care of Alice the Cat who will take care of the rats. Give him something for her!

KING. A pouch of gold!

MENDENHALL. Well, I…

73

Plays for Children

QUEEN. *(Cutting in.)* A pouch of gold is not enough for this wonderful animal!

KING. Well—maybe two pouches!

MENDENHALL. Two pouches?

QUEEN. I told you, husband, don't be stingy!

KING. This is why the budget never balances!

MENDENHALL. But, surely, your majesty...

QUEEN. Don't bring up that budget now! You know perfectly well we can tax more if we need it. Just think of the savings on food alone!

KING. I know, my dear, but we've got to think of the money, too.

> *(He is interrupted by the re-entry of the RATS and CAT. Again, in dance, there is a chase, ending in the exit of all RATS and CAT.)*

QUEEN. Do you need another demonstration? You should be ready to pay any price!

KING. If you will just be quiet, the captain and I can get down to business!

MENDENHALL. Of course, your majesty, I am most anxious to trade. The young lad in London, Dick Whittington, ventured his all on this.

KING. Well, well, we'll see. Ho, servants! *(One appears.)* Bring in that chest of diamonds that stands in the hall. *(SERVANT exits.)* Perhaps, Captain, you will find this suitable. *(Two SERVANTS re-enter carrying a large, obviously heavy chest.)* There you are, Captain, a whole chest full of diamonds for the cat.

MENDENHALL. 'Tis a worthy offer, your majesty, but still, I rather think Alice might do you more good than all the diamonds.

KING. This, of course, is in addition to the two pouches of gold

MENDENHALL. Ah, yes, of course. Yet, when you figure what the rats cost you each year...

QIEEN. I must have this cat, no matter what the costs This ring— *(drawing from finger)*—is a pure emerald. This I will give!

KING. And another chest, this time full of gold. Servants! *(The two SERVANTS exit and return with another chest, equally heavy.)* Gold I can get whenever I need it!

MENDENHALL. But a cat is a rarity in this kingdom.

KING. 'Tis the truth. Well, then, I'll throw in this. *(Removes a heavy medallion from around neck.)* Your Dick Whittington will find this almost of more value than all the rest put together!

MENDENHALL. Done! *(Shakes hands.)* 'Tis a rare bargain you have made your majesty! You will never regret it—and you have made the fortune of a deserving lad!

(CAT bounds in, preening and cleaning. KING and QUEEN approach her cautiously, finally screwing up enough courage to stroke her. Cat and KING and QUEEN beam.)

QUEEN. Nice Cat. Such soft fur!

CAT. Meowr! ("This is the life.")

(The lights dim to black.)

ACT II

Scene 3

The street.

PLANKY and GAUNT sidle on with many a backward glance.

PLANKY. You're really gonna do it?

GAUNT. Arrh! 'Course I am. There plenty gold in that house fer the taken' and I'm the bloke to take it! No more of this cut-purse work!

PLANKY. Yes, but what about the big-un? Won't 'e want his cut?

GAUNT. *(Fiercely.)* An' what if he does? We're the ones doin' the work, we're the one what gets the gold. Besides, he don't need to know nuffin about it!

PLANKY. 'E's everywhere. 'E'd sure find out!

GAUNT. Not if we don't tell 'em, see. Just you an' me! I won't say nuffin' and—*(drawing dagger)*—so iff'n he finds out, you'd be the only one what could have told 'em. *(Threatening.)* Now, are ye with me er not?

PLANKY. *(Backing away from the knife.)* Oh, I'm with you, I'm just as sick as you are of 'is ways. We does all the work an' takes 'is cut,

GAUNT. 'Tain't gonna be that way no more! *(Sheathing dagger.)* How, 'ere's what we'll do: You goes up to the scullery door an' pretends to be sick. I'll be holdin' you up, an' tellin' 'em how you fainted an'

Plays for Children

would they please give you a bite to eat. Then, when they lets us in we knock 'em in the 'ead an' takes what we wants.

PLANKY. S'pose there's more'n one?

GAUNT. Then we knock 'em both in the 'ead! But there won't be. I seen the master o' the house drivin' off with that goody-goody daughter o' his'n just a little while ago. That means there's only the cook an' that scullery boy!

PLANKY. I don't like it.

GAUNT. Wot are ye, lily-livered?

PLANKY. Nah! It's just that I ain't never done nuttin' like this.

GAUNT. Well, y'r gotta learn sometimes. Now come on!

(The two exit, PLANKY lagging.)

ACT II

Scene 4

The scullery.

COOK runs in, screaming.

COOK. Help, help! A rat is chasing me! *(Dives under the table.)*

DICK. *(Running in opposite, snatches broom.)* Don't worry cook. I'll take care of it! *(Rushes out.)*

COOK. *(Still under table, shouting.)* Arrah! And if you hadn't been so selfish and sent that cat to the Spice Islands, we wouldn't have this problem. *(Crawls out.)* I never seen such a boy! Here I takes him in and feeds him and his cat, and the first thing he does is send her away. Then he's always cuddlin' up to the master like he was gooder' than gold! Bah!

DICK. *(Entering.)* I couldn't find any rat, Cook.

COOK. Now he's telling me there wasn't any rat when I seen it with my own two eyes!

DICK. No, honestly, Cook. I went down the hall, same way as you came, and I thought I saw it, too. But when I crept up on it, I saw it was just a shadow. It did look like a rat, though.

COOK. Are you calling me a liar?

DICK. No, no, of course not. Anybody would have been fooled by it.

Plays for Children

COOK. 'Twas a rat I saw an' any insolent, dirty Lunnon beggar who tells me I'm lying had better watch out! *(Chases DICK.)*

DICK. *(Dodging easily.)* Cook, you're getting old and can't catch me any more!

COOK. Old, is it. I'll show you! *(Chases him out, then waddles back to table.)* Old, bah! *(Resumes working at table. There is a knock at the door.)* Now who could that be? Some tradesman, I'll be bound!

(Opens the door, revealing PLANKY supported by GAUNT.)

GAUNT. Please, ma'am, my friend here has fainted. Would ye by any chance 'have a bit of hot soup?

COOK. Aarrgh! Begone wid ye! I've got no soup for beggars such as ye! I've seen the likes of you before!

GAUNT. But my friend 'as fainted!

COOK. 'Tis no worry o' mine! Now clear out, the both of you!

(She starts to close door. GAUHT puts his foot in way and shoulders in.)

GAUNT. I knew a fine looking lass like yerself would not be turning us away—or you'd better not! *(PLANKY suddenly straightens up. GAUHT draws a dagger, advances on her.)* Y' see, my nice little friend here *(the dagger)* is hungry and he likes to drink. I don't give him any—usually *(a jab at her)* and if you're quiet, I won't right now!

COOK. *(Terrified.)* What do you want?

GAUNT. Like I told you, my friend 'ere wants some hot soup.

(Both PLANKY and GAUHT have their backs to DICK'S entrance. During the next action, as PLANKY and GAUHT are backing COOK across the room, he comes in, sizes up the situation, seizes a stick from the woodbox, and stalks the pair.)

PLANKY. Yeah—soup with gold in it!

GAUNT. That's right! That's the kind of soup that is healthiest. Now, are you gonna tells where it is or are we gonna feed my little friend here? *(He waggles his dagger.)*

COOK. Sure but I ain't got anything.

GAUNT. We knows that—but we also knows you knows where it's kept! An' we want it, see!

(DICK swings stick on GAUNT, hitting him a glancing blow that staggers him but does not knock him out. COOK screams. PLANKY takes a swift look, and flees out the door. DICK and GAUHT circle, COOK cowers in

Plays for Children

the corner, vocalizing. DICK swings his stick again as GAUNT thrusts at him with the dagger. The blow catches GAUHT on his extended arm, knocking the dagger away.)

DICK. Now you've not got your dagger, bully boy. *(Dropping stick.)* Mayhaps you'd like to try it fair and square.

(He advances threateningly on GAUNT who stands briefly, then flees out of the door.)

COOK. I knew it'd happen, I knew it would!

DICK. Maybe I should call the watch—knew what would happen, Cook?

COOK. That sooner er later your gang would try to get in her an' steal us blind!

DICK. *(Dumbfounded.)* My gang? But Cook, you just saw me chase them out. And a good thing too that I was here.

COOK. Aye, an thim robbers knew it, too, knew just when to come— an' only one person in the house would tell them—you!

DICK. Me? But I...

(He is interrupted by ALICE'S entrance.)

ALICE. Cook, we got back earlier than we thought, and Father would like to see you.

COOK. Aargh, now, an' I can feel it in my bones that something else haf happened. *(Exits.)*

ALICE. What's the matter with her?

DICK. Oh, well...

ALICE. I know, she's always like that. Does she still bully you?

DICK. Maybe not as bad as she used to, but she just doesn't seem to trust me. Lady Alice, has something happened?

ALICE. I don't know. Father has been acting awfully worried about something the last few days. I heard him say something about pirates and Captain Mendenhall but I...

DICK. Pirates? Has something happened to the ship? Did pirates get her?

ALICE. I don't know, Dick, I don't know anything. But let's not worry about that now. Tell me, have you been studying your reading?

DICK. Oh, yes, every night—that is, when Cook lets me. I take a candle to my room, but if Cook sees the candle, she takes it away from me. Says we can't afford to waste candles on the likes o' me.

ALICE. *(Indignant.)* What business is it of hers? They're our candles—but never mind, Dick. You just keep at it; you've got to be able to read well if you're going to make your fortune. Why don't you get the book right now and show me?

DICK. All right. *(Goes to woodbox and slides a small book from behind it.)* Cook never thinks of looking behind the box. If she did, she'd burn the book.

ALICE. Never mind. Let me hear you.

DICK. *(Reading hesitantly.)* "A mer-chant, to be successful, must keep an am-ple supply of goods and must keep sharp ac-counts of what he has. He should be di…di…" Oh, I can't make out those long words!

ALICE. *(Encouraging.)* Oh, yes you can now Dick, it isn't that hard. Sound it out.

DICK. Di-li-gent. Diligent. What does it mean?

ALICE. It means he works hard and keeps at it. Now go on.

DICK. *(Smoother.)* "He should be diligent, but always thoughtful of his assistants." *(COOK has entered, dejected and weeping.)* Why, Cook, what's the matter?

ALICE. Cook, why are you crying? What's the matter?

COOK. Matter enough, your Ladyship. Your father was just tellin' me the "Bonaventure" has been took by pirates an' that we'll never be seeing hide nor hair of our ventures again.

ALICE. Oh, no, he didn't.

COOK. Oh, yes, he did. He said that another ship had docked and reported the "Bonaventure" captured.

ALICE. Why didn't that ship help the "Bonaventure?"

COOK. Sure, now, and a smart captain stays away from pirates. Oooooh, why wasn't Captain Mendenhall that smart!

DICK. Then Alice is at the bottom of the sea. Alice—she was all I had—I'll never see her again.

COOK. Wurra, wurra! What'll ee do now?

ALICE. Do? Why, we'll start over, that's what we'll do. I'm going to talk to Father right now.

(She turns, bumps into FITZWARREN entering.)

Plays for Children

FITZWARREN. Now I know I shall buy you a trumpet. Or would you rather have Dick here walk ahead of you with a red lantern to warn people of your approach?

DICK. Mr. Fitzwarren, is it true the "Bonaventure" has been taken?

FITZWAREN. Then Cook has told you. The report is not yet confirmed, but it looks very much like it, lad, and it's truly sorry I am for you.

DICK. But you have lost more than I, sir.

FITZWARREN. Your venture was as valuable to you as my whole shipload to me.

DICK. Aye.

(He turns away to hide his feeling.)

ALICE. But Father, can't we send out another venture?

FITZWARREN. Of course, and we will—but first we've got to find another ship and another reliable captain.

COOK. 'Tis bad luck that spalpeen has brought to this household. Dick, I mean.

FITZWARREN. Cook, that is no way to talk!

COOK. Beggin' yer pardon, sir, but I've got to say what I've got to say. First, we never had a rat in this household 'till he come. Then, all of a sudden we have 'em; one just chased me down the hall. You never lost a venture in all these years, but as soon as he sends his cat, down it all goes to the bottom of the sea.

ALICE. Oh, Father, don't let her talk like that!

COOK. And then, finally, just today, I was attacked in me own scullery by two of his gang! Oh, he pretended to fight them and drive them away, but they really was in cahoots!

FITZWARREN. That will do! We'll have no talk like that, Cook—and if we do, I shall see that you regret it! Come Alice, we must go.

(Exits with ALICE, who glances sadly back at a dispirited DICK, sitting on the woodbox with head in hands.)

COOK. *(Ominously.)* So you've bewitched him, too!

DICK. Bewitched him?

COOK. Aye, bewitched. You've been tellin' us all along that you're not a Lunnon beggar, fighting and brawling with a gang of guttersnipes. But you beat the tallest and strongest of 'em and made him run.

You've got Lady Alice and Mr. Fitzwarren right in the palm of your hand so you can do no wrong and you've got the run o' the house, you, a scullery lad! So it's a witch you are for sure!

DICK. I don't know what you're talking about.

COOK. *(Venomously.)* Ye don't, eh? And I suppose that cat of yours wasn't a witch's cat neither.

(She advances on DICK.)

DICK. Alice was no witch's cat.

COOK. Bah! I've seen 'em often enough in Ireland! You made a fine pair, cozening the Fitzwarrens, an' livin' off the fat of the land!

DICK. That's not true! I've worked hard here, and you know it!

COOK. *(Picking up meat cleaver.)* I know it, do I? An' I know about witches and their cats. Many's the time I've seen witches riding their brooms with their cats sitting on their shoulders. It's a wonder it didn't dawn on me until now that you and that cat put the evil eye on this household. Well, I'm going to fix you now that Lady Alice and Mr. Fitzwarren ain't here!

(COOK advances on DICK who realizes she is in earnest, and finally manages to escape outside with COOK. COOK re-enters, tossing cleaver on table.)

COOK. That takes care of the likes o' him. This household is well rid o' Dick Whittington and his cat.

(She exits. The lights dim to black.)

ACT II

Scene 5

The scullery.

In the darkness the church bells come up and then go under the VOICE.

VOICE. Turn back, Turn back, Dick Whittington, Thrice Lord Mayor of London.

(The bells fade down and under the first of the next line. Lights come up on the scullery as ALICE runs on.)

ALICE. Dick—the church bells of St. Mary-le-bow. They're saying something. *(Listening intently.)* Turn back, Turn back, Dick Whittington, Thrice Lord Mayor of London. Dick, Dick, where are you? Can you hear what the bells are saying? *(COOK enters.)* Oh, Cook, where is Dick?

Plays for Children

COOK. Somewhere's around, I guess.

(*The voice and bells fade out.*)

ALICE. I thought I heard the church bells pealing his name.

COOK. Church bells pealing his name—he really has you bewitched, Lady Alice! I heard nothing but the bells of St. Mary-le-bow.

ALICE. Maybe he's in his room. (*Exits.*)

COOK. (*Satisfied.*) No, he ain't in his room. He ain't anywhere around if I know anything—and I know a lot about the likes o' him.

ALICE. (*Entering.*) He's not there, Cook. Something's happened to him. I know it!

COOK. Oh, come now, Lady Alice, nothin's happened to him. Why, you can't hurt a Lunnon beggar boy!

ALICE. (*Angry.*) He's not a beggar boy! Some day he'll be someone important—and when that day comes, you'd better be careful.

COOK. Not 'alf likely! Just because he loses his venture he runs away. Hah!

ALICE. Runs away? What makes you say he ran away?

COOK. (*Flustered.*) Oh—I—well, I don't know he's run off. It's just if he ain't here, he's somewhere else. And where else but with that gang of his?

ALICE. You drove him away, didn't you? Yes you did! You never liked him from the minute we found him fainting out there. What have you done to him?

FITZWARREN. (*Entering.*) There you are, Alice. I've teen looking all over.

ALICE. (*Running to him.*) Father, Father, Dick is gone!

FITZWARREN. Are you sure?

ALICE. Absolutely! I've looked everywhere. (*Sharply.*) And Cook drove him away! I know it!

COOK. (*Unctuously.*) Why, Mr. Fitzwarren, sir, I wouldn't drive out the dear lad. Why, I loved him like me own son! Sure, an' 'tis overwrought the dear child is!

ALICE. I am not. I don't know what she did or how she did it, but just as sure as I'm standing here, she's done some evil to Dick.

Plays for Children

FITZWARREN. There, now, I'm sure he'll turn up—and you are excited.

ALIVE. I am not! This old Cook...

COOK. *(Whining.)* Now, Mr. Fitzwarren, I've been with you these many years and I've taken care of the family like it was my own, especially since Lady Fitzwarren died. *(In shocked disbelief.)* Why, here he is now.

(ALL turn as DICK enters. During following scene COOK goes outdoors, unnoticed by others.)

ALICE. Dick! Dick, where have you been?

DICK. Oh, I just took a little walk. I didn't feel very well after hearing about the "Bonaventure."

FITZWARREN. *(Comforting.)* I didn't feel very well about it myself. But, lad, we can't worry about what is past.

DICK. I know that now, sir. The important thing is to keep trying,

FITZWARREN. Then you have learned a good lesson. Alice, my girl, you worried over nothing. Mark my words, this lad will rise to high places some day. Mayhap even lord mayor of London! *(Exits.)*

DICK. *(To himself, shock.)* Lord Mayor of London!

ALICE. Dick, what's the matter? You look as though you'd seen a ghost.

DICK. *(Turning to her.)* Lady Alice, I didn't go for a walk. I was really running away—going back home. Cook had called me a witch, and tried to hurt me with that meat cleaver. London was no place for me, my venture had been lost—and—well, I was almost out of the city at Highgate when the strangest thing happened. I heard the bells of St. Mary-le-bow. They seemed to say, "Turn back, turn back, Dick Whittington, Thrice Lord Mayor of London."

ALICE. You heard them, too?

DICK. And just now, when your father said...

ALICE. *(As though announcing.)* The Lord Mayor of London. *(Curtsies.)*

DICK. Don't make fun of me, Lady Alice.

ALICE. Oh, but I'm not. Some day you will be lord mayor and ride in a golden carriage! Oh, I must tell Father. And I'll tell him about Cook attacking you, too! *(Exits.)*

DICK. Lady Alice, don't—maybe it was just a dream. *(But she is gone.)* Dick Whittington, thrice lord mayor—three times lord mayor! I couldn't have been hearing things. Lady Alice said she heard them,

Plays for Children

too. And church bells wouldn't be telling a lie, they couldn't and be church bells. But look at me, just a scullery boy, with nothing to my name, not even a cat. How can I ever amount to anything, much less become lord mayor? Well, at least I didn't let that old Cook get the best of me. So, I might as well do my work.

(DICK begins to clean the fireplace. When his back is to the door, COOK enters with GAUNT. She points toward DICK, then stands to one side. GAUNT draws his dagger and stalks DICK, dropping behind the table when DICK half turns and resumes stalk when DICK'S back again is turned. Just as he raises the dagger to stab him, DICK turns, takes in the situation, and grapples with GAUNT. There is a see-saw fight, with DICK gradually being beaten and forced to the floor.)

MENDENHALL. *(Off.)* Dick! Dick Whittington

COOK. Begorrs! It's Captain Mendenhall!

GAUNT. Block the door!

(DICK seizes the opportunity of this momentary diversion to disarm and pins GAUNT.)

MENDENHALL. *(Entering.)* Dick, I've traded… *(Drawing sword.)* What's going on here? What are you two up to?

(FITZWARREN and ALICE enter.)

DICK. I know not. This man jumped me with his dagger. I was but defending myself.

FITZWARREN. Was he going to steal something?

COOK. Sure, an' that's it. They're in cahoots together. I told you he'd bring in his gang. This is one o' them!

GAUNT. Don't listen to that old trollop! She hired me to do 'im in. Would have, too, in a half a mo'!

(COOK bolts for the door. ALICE attempts to grab her and is shoved aside violently. FITZWARREN makes the capture as COOK is almost out.)

ALICE. She's hated him ever since he came, Father.

COOK. *(Malevolently.)* Aye, that I have! And why not! He's a witch, a warlock who put an evil eye on the "Boaaventure" and she went to the bottom of the sea with all our ventures.

MENDENHALL. *(Who is holding GAUNT.)* But that he did not! I traded all our ventures to the King of the Spice Islands. Dick's cat was just what he needed to rid his castle of rats, and I drove a roaring trade. Dick is wealthy. Ho, there lads! Bring in the chests.

Plays for Children

(SAILORS *carry in Dick's chests. Ad lib exclamations.*)

MENDEHHALL. There you are, lad! By courtesy of Alice the Cat!

DICK. *(Dazed.)* All—mine?

FITZWARREN. All yours, honestly ventured and honestly gained.

MEHDENHALL. In fact, we're all rich. 'Twas the most successful voyage I ever have made!

COOK. And my venture?

ALICE. Father, she shouldn't get anything, she's been so mean!

FITZWARREN. She must get what is come to her—but I'll see that she gets it in a nice, quiet jail!

MEHDENHALL. Bos'n, take these two to the Newgate gare where they belong!

SAILOR. Aye, aye, sir. Bear a hand, there lads!

(*SAILORS exit with COOK and GAUMT as prisoners.*)

COOK. *(As she is forced off.)* You can't get away with this! You haven't heard the last from me!

(They are gone.)

FATHER. And now, Captain, you must tell me the events of voyage over a bottle of port.

(He glances significantly toward DICK and ALICE. MENDENHALL takes his meaning.)

MEHDENHALL. Aye. 'Tis a tale that will not interest the young people. Well, all went smoothly 'til we rounded the cape...

(They are out.)

ALICE. Well, Dick, what do you say now?

DICK. *(Still dazed.)* I cannot believe it. All this for Alice!

ALICE. Which Alice are you speaking of, sir? I or the cat?

DICK. The cat—oh, and you, too, your ladyship. Had it not been for your urging, I would have ventured nothing.

ALICE. And now, sir, perhaps you will listen while the Bow Bells speak. Dick Whittington, Thrice Lord Mayor of London!

(ALICE curtsies deeply. DICK, taken aback, sees her curtsy, and gets the idea. He takes a large pendant from the jewel chest, places it on his neck. He then places a huge jewelled ring on his finger. He then brushes off his rags,

Plays for Children

straightens them, and walking very regally, indeed, walks over to ALICE, extending his hand, which she takes. He pulls her up to her feet as the bells of St. Mary-le-Bow peal triumphantly.)

End of Play

Plays for Children

THE PRINCESS AND THE WOODCUTTER

by A. A. Milne

Characters

Woodcutter
Princess
King
Queen
Red Prince
Blue Prince
Yellow Prince

The WOODCUTTER is discovered singing at his work, in a glade of the forest outside his hut. He is tall and strong, and brave and handsome; all that a woodcutter ought to be. Now it happened that the PRINCESS was passing, and as soon as his song is finished, sure enough, on she comes.

PRINCESS. Good morning, Woodcutter.

WOODCUTTER. Good morning. *(But he goes on with his work.)*

PRINCESS. *(After a pause.)* Good morning, Woodcutter.

WOODCUTTER. Good morning.

PRINCESS. Don't you ever say anything except good morning?

WOODCUTTER. Sometimes I say good-bye.

PRINCESS. You *are* a cross woodcutter today.

WOODCUTTER. I have work to do.

PRINCESS. You are still cutting wood? Don't you ever do anything else?

WOODCUTTER. Well, you are still a Princess; don't *you* ever do anything else?

Plays for Children

PRINCESS. *(Reproachfully.)* Now, that's not fair, Woodcutter. You can't say I was a Princess yesterday, when I came and helped you stack your wood. Or the day before, when I tied up your hand where you had cut it. Or the day before that, when we had our meal together on the grass. Was I a Princess then?

WOODCUTTER. Somehow I think you were. Somehow I think you were saying to yourself, "Isn't it sweet of a Princess to treat a mere woodcutter like this?"

PRINCESS. I think you're perfectly horrid. I've a good mind never to speak to you again. And—and I would, if only I could be sure that you would notice I wasn't speaking to you.

WOODCUTTER. After all, I'm just as bad as you. Only yesterday I was thinking to myself how unselfish I was to interrupt my work in order to talk to a mere Princess.

PRINCESS. Yes, but the trouble is that you *don't* interrupt your work.

WOODCUTTER. *(Interrupting it and going up to her with a smile.)* Madam, I am at your service.

PRINCESS. I wish I thought you were.

WOODCUTTER. Surely you have enough people at your service already. Princes and Chancellors and Chamberlains and Waiting Maids.

PRINCESS. Yes, that's just it. That's why I want your help. Particularly in the matter of the Princes.

WOODCUTTER. Why, has a suitor come for the hand of her Royal Highness?

PRINCESS. Three suitors. And I hate them all.

WOODCUTTER. And which are you going to marry?

PRINCESS. I don't know. Father hasn't made up his mind yet.

WOODCUTTER. And this is a matter which father—which His Majesty decides for himself?

PRINCESS. Why, of course! You should read the History Books, Woodcutter. The suitors to the hand of a Princess are always set some trial of strength or test of quality by the King, and the winner marries his daughter.

WOODCUTTER. Well, I don't live in a Palace, and I think my own thoughts about these things. I'd better get back to my work. *(He goes on with his chopping.)*

Plays for Children

PRINCESS. *(Gently, after a pause.)* Woodcutter!

WOODCUTTER. *(Looking up.)* Oh, are you there? I thought you were married by this time.

PRINCES. *(Meekly.)* I don't want to be married. *(Hastily.)* I mean, not to any of those three.

WOODCUTTER. You can't help yourself.

PRINCESS. I know. That's why I wanted *you* to help me.

WOODCUTTER. Can a simple woodcutter help a Princess?

PRINCESS. Well, perhaps a simple one couldn't, but a clever one might.

WOODCUTTER. What would his reward be?

PRINCESS. His reward would be that the Princess, not being married to any of her three suitors, would still be able to help him chop his wood in the mornings. I *am* helping you, aren't I?

WOODCUTTER. *(Smiling.)* Oh, decidedly.

PRINCESS. *(Nodding.)* I thought I was.

WOODCUTTER. It is kind of a great lady like yourself to help so humble a fellow as I.

PRINCESS. I'm not *very* great. *(And she isn't. She is the smallest, daintiest little Princess that ever you saw.)*

WOODCUTTER. There's enough of you to make a hundred men unhappy.

PRINCESS. And one man happy?

WOODCUTTER. And one man very, very happy.

PRINCESS. *(Innocently.)* I wonder who he'll be….Woodcutter, if *you* were a Prince, would you be my suitor?

WOODCUTTER. *(Scornfully.)* One of three?

PRINCESS. *(Excitedly.)* Oo, would you kill the others? With that axe?

WOODCUTTER. I would not kill them, in order to help His Majesty make up his mind about his son-in-law. But if the Princess had made up her mind—and wanted me…

PRINCESS. Yes?

WOODCUTTER. Then I would marry her, however many suitors she had.

PRINCESS. Well, she's only got three at present.

Plays for Children

WOODCUTTER. What is that to me?

PRINCESS. Oh, I just thought you might want to be doing something to your axe.

WOODCUTTER. My axe?

PRINCESS. Yes. You see, she *has* made up her mind.

WOODCUTTER. *(Amazed.)* You mean—But—but I'm only a woodcutter.

PRINCESS. That's where you'll have the advantage of them, when it comes to axes.

WOODCUTTER. Princess! *(He takes her in his arms.)* My Princess!

PRINCESS. Woodcutter! My woodcutter! My, oh so very slow and uncomprehending, but entirely adorable woodcutter!

(They sing together. They just happen to feel like that.)

WOODCUTTER. *(The song finished.)* But what will His Majesty say?

PRINCESS. All sorts of things. Do you really love me, woodcutter, or have I proposed to you under a misapprehension?

WOODCUTTER. I adore you!

PRINCESS. I thought you did. But I wanted to hear you say it. If I had been a simple peasant, I suppose you would have said it a long time ago?

WOODCUTTER. I expect so.

PRINCESS. Yes....Well, now we must think of a plan for making Mother like you.

WOODCUTTER. Might I just kiss you again before we begin?

PRINCESS. Well, I don't quite see how I am to stop you.

(The WOODCUTTER picks her up in his arms and kisses her.)

WOODCUTTER. There!

PRINCESS. *(In his arms.)* Oh, Woodcutter, woodcutter, why didn't you do that the first day I saw you? Then I needn't have had the bother of proposing to you. *(He puts her down suddenly.)* What is it?

WOODCUTTER. Somebody coming. *(He peers through the trees and then says in surprise:)* The King!

PRINCESS. Oh! I must fly!

WOODCUTTER. But you'll come back?

PRINCESS. Perhaps.

(She disappears quickly through the trees. The WOODCUTTER goes on with his work and is discovered at it a minute later by the KING and QUEEN.)

KING. *(Puffing.)* Ah! and a seat all ready for us. How satisfying. *(They sit down, a distinguished couple—reading from left to right, "KING, QUEEN"—on a bench outside the WOODCUTTER'S hut.)*

QUEEN. *(Crossly—she was like that.)* I don't know why you dragged me here.

KING. As I told you, my love, to be alone.

QUEEN. Well, you aren't alone.

(She indicates the WOODCUTTER.)

KING. Pooh, he doesn't matter. Well now, about these three Princes. They are getting on my mind rather. It is time we decided which one of them is to marry our beloved child. The trouble is to choose between them.

QUEEN. As regards appetite, there is nothing to choose between them. They are three of the heartiest eaters I have met for some time.

KING. You are right. The sooner we choose one of them, and send the other two about their business, the better. *(Reflectively.)* There were six peaches on the breakfast-table this morning. Did I get one? No.

QUEEN. Did *I* get one? No.

KING. Did our darling child get one—not that it matters? No.

QUEEN. It is a pity that the seven-headed bull died last year.

KING. Yes, he had a way of sorting out competitors for the hand of our beloved one that was beyond all praise. One could have felt quite sure that, had the three competitors been introduced to him, only one of them would have taken any further interest in the matter.

QUEEN. *(Always the housekeeper.)* And even he mightn't have taken any interest in his meals.

KING. *(With a sigh.)* However, those days are over. We must think of a new test. Somehow I think that, in a son-in-law, moral worth is even more to be desired than mere brute strength. Now my suggestion is this: that you should disguise yourself as a beggar woman and approach each of the three princes in turn, supplicating their charity. In this way we shall discover which of the three has the kindest heart. What do you say, my dear?

Plays for Children

QUEEN. An excellent plan. If you remember, I suggested it myself yesterday.

KING. *(Annoyed.)* Well, of course, it had been in my mind for some time. I don't claim that the idea is original; it has often been done in our family. *(Getting up.)* Well then, if you will get ready, my dear, I will go and find our three friends and see that they come this way.

(They go out together. As soon as they are out of sight the PRINCESS comes back.)

PRINCESS. Well, Woodcutter, what did I tell you?

WOODCUTTER. What did you tell me?

PRINCESS. Didn't you listen to what they said?

WOODCUTTER. I didn't listen, but I couldn't help hearing.

PRINCESS. Well, *I* couldn't help listening. And unless you stop it somehow, I shall be married to one of them to-night.

WOODCUTTER. Which one?

PRINCESS. The one with the kindest heart—whichever that is.

WOODCUTTER. Supposing they all three have kind hearts?

PRINCESS. *(Confidently.)* They won't. They never have. In our circles when three Princes come together, one of them has a kind heart and the other two haven't. *(Surprised.)* Haven't you read any History at all?

WOODCUTTER. I have no time for reading. But I think it's time History was altered a little. We'll alter it this afternoon.

PRINCESS. What do you mean?

WOODCUTTER. Leave this to me. I've got an idea.

PRINCESS. *(Clapping her hands.)* Oh, how clever of you! But what do you want me to do?

WOODCUTTER. *(Pointing.)* You know the glade over there where the brook runs through it? Wait for me there.

PRINCESS. I obey my lord's commands.

(The WOODCUTTER resumes his work. By and by the RED PRINCE comes along. He is a—well, you will see for yourself what he is like.)

RED PRINCE. Ah, fellow....Fellow...I said fellow! *(Yes, that sort of man.)*

WOODCUTTER. *(Looking up.)* Were you speaking to me, my lord?

RED PRINCE. There is no other fellow here that I can see.

Plays for Children

(The WOODCUTTER looks round to make sure, peers behind a tree or two, and comes back to the PRINCE.)

WOODCUTTER. Yes, you must have meant me.

RED PRINCE. Yes, of course I meant you, fellow. Have you seen the Princess come past this way? I was told she was waiting for me here.

WOODCUTTER. She is not here, my lord. *(Looking round to see that they are alone.)* My lord, are you one of the Princes who is seeking the hand of the Princess.

RED PRINCE. *(Complacently.)* I am, fellow.

WOODCUTTER. His Majesty the King was here a while ago. He is to make his decision between you this afternoon. *(Meaningly.)* I think I can help you to be the lucky one, my lord.

RED PRINCE. You suggest that I take an unfair advantage over my fellow-competitors?

WOODCUTTER. I suggest nothing, my lord. I only say that I can help you.

RED PRINCE. *(Magnanimously.)* Well, I will allow you to help me.

WOODCUTTER. Thank you. Then I will give you this advice. If a beggar woman asks you for a crust of bread this afternoon, remember—it is the test!

RED PRINCE. *(Staggered.)* The test! But I haven't *got* a crust of bread!

WOODCUTTER. Wait here and I will get you one. *(He goes into the hut.)*

RED PRINCE. *(Speaking after him as he goes.)* My good fellow, I am extremely obliged to you, and if ever I can do anything for you, such as returning a crust to you of similar size, or even lending you another slightly smaller one, or…*(The WOODCUTTER comes back with the crust.)* Ah, thank you, my man, thank you.

WOODCUTTER. I would suggest, my lord, that you should take a short walk in this direction *(pointing to the opposite direction to that which the* **PRINCESS** *has taken)* and stroll back casually in a few minutes' time when the Queen is here.

RED PRINCE. Thank you, my man, thank you.

(He puts the crust in his pocket and goes off. The WOODCUTTER goes on with his work. The BLUE PRINCE comes in and stands watching him in silence for some moments.)

WOODCUTTER. *(Looking up.)* Hullo!

93

Plays for Children

BLUE PRINCE. Hullo!

WOODCUTTER. What do you want?

BLUE PRINCE. The Princess.

WOODCUTTER. She's not here.

BLUE PRINCE. Oh!

>   *(The WOODCUTTER goes on with his work and the BLUE PRINCE goes on looking at him.)*

WOODCUTTER. *(Struck with an idea.)* Are you one of the Princes who is wooing the Princess?

BLUE PRINCE. Yes.

WOODCUTTER. I believe I could help your Royal Highness.

BLUE PRINCE. Do.

WOODCUTTER. *(Doubtfully.)* It would perhaps be not quite fair to the others.

BLUE PRINCE. Don't mind.

WOODCUTTER. Well then, listen.

>   *(WOODCUTTER pauses a moment and looks round to see that they are alone.)*

BLUE PRINCE. I'm listening.

WOODCUTTER. If you come back in five minutes, you will see a beggar woman sitting here. She will ask you for a crust of bread. You must give it to her, for it is the way His Majesty has chosen of testing your kindness of heart.

BLUE PRINCE. *(Feeling in his pockets.)* No bread.

WOODCUTTER. I will give you some.

BLUE PRINCE. Do.

WOODCUTTER. *(Taking a piece from his pocket.)* Here you are.

BLUE PRINCE. Thanks.

WOODCUTTER. Not at all, I'm very glad to have been able to help you.

>   *(WOODCUTTER goes on with his work. The BLUE PRINCE remains looking at him.)*

BLUE PRINCE. *(With a great effort.)* Thanks.

(He goes slowly away. A moment later the YELLOW PRINCE makes a graceful and languid entry.)

YELLOW PRINCE. Ah, come hither, my man, come hither.

WOODCUTTER. *(Stopping his work and looking up.)* You want me, sir?

YELLOW PRINCE. Come hither, my man. Tell me, has her Royal Highness the Princess passed this way lately?

WOODCUTTER. The Princess?

YELLOW PRINCE. Yes, the Princess, my bumpkin. But perhaps you have been too much concerned in your own earthy affairs to have noticed her. You—ah—cut wood, I see.

WOODCUTTER. Yes, sir, I am a woodcutter.

YELLOW PRINCE. A most absorbing life. Some day we must have a long talk about it. But just now I have other business waiting for me. With your permission, good friend, I will leave you to your chopping. *(He starts to go.)*

WOODCUTTER. Beg your pardon, sir, but are you one of those Princes that want to marry our Princess?

YELLOW PRINCE. I had hoped, good friend, to obtain your permission to do so. I beg you not to refuse it.

WOODCUTTER. You are making fun of me, sir.

YELLOW PRINCE. Discerning creature.

WOODCUTTER. All the same, I *can* help you.

YELLOW PRINCE. Then pray do so, log-chopper, and earn my everlasting gratitude.

WOODCUTTER. The King has decided that whichever of you three Princes has the kindest heart shall marry his daughter.

YELLOW PRINCE. Then you will be able to bear witness to him that I have already wasted several minutes of my valuable time in condescending to a mere wood-splitter. Tell him this and the prize is mine. *(Kissing the tips of his fingers.)* Princess, I embrace you.

WOODCUTTER. The King will not listen to me. But if you return here in five minutes, you will find an old woman begging for bread. It is the test which their Majesties have arranged for you. If you share your last crust with her…

YELLOW PRINCE. Yes, but do I look as if I carried a last crust about with me?

Plays for Children

WOODCUTTER. But see, I will give you one.

YELLOW PRINCE. *(Taking it between the tips of his fingers.)* Yes, but...

WOODCUTTER. Put it in your pocket, and when...

YELLOW PRINCE. But, my dear bark-scraper, have you no feeling for clothes at all? How can I put a thing like this in my pocket? *(Handing it back to him.)* I beg you to wrap it up. Here take this. *(Gives him a scarf.)* Neatly, I pray you. *(Taking an orange ribbon out of his pocket.)* Perhaps a little of this round it would make it more tolerable. You think so? I leave it to you. I trust your *taste entirely*. Leaving a loop for the little finger, I entreat you...so. *(He hangs it on his little finger.)* In about five minutes, you said? We will be there. *(With a bow.)* We thank you.

> *(He departs delicately. The WOODCUTTER smiles to himself, puts down his axe and goes off to the PRINCESS. And just in time. For behold! the KING and QUEEN return. At least we think it is the QUEEN, but she is so heavily disguised by a cloak which she wears over her court dress, that for a moment we are not quite sure.)*

KING. Now then, my love, if you will sit down on that log there—*(Placing her.)* Excellent—I think perhaps you should remove the crown. *(Removes it.)* There! Now the disguise is perfect.

QUEEN. You're sure they are coming? It's a very uncomfortable seat.

KING. I told them that the Princess was waiting for them here. Their natural disappointment at finding I was mistaken will make the test of their good nature an even more exacting one. My own impression is that the Yellow Prince will be the victor.

QUEEN. Oh, I hate that man.

KING. *(Soothingly.)* Well, well, perhaps it will be the Blue one.

QUEEN. If anything, I dislike him *more* intensely.

KING. Or even the Red.

QUEEN. Ugh! I can't bear him.

KING. Fortunately, dear, you are not called upon to marry any of them. It is for our darling that we are making the great decision. Listen! I hear one coming. I will hide in the cottage and take note of what happens.

> *(He disappears into the cottage as the BLUE PRINCE comes in.)*

QUEEN. Oh, sir, can you kindly spare a crust of bread for a poor old woman! Please, pretty gentleman!

Plays for Children

BLUE PRINCE. *(Standing stolidly in front of her and feeling in his pocket.)* Bread…Bread…Ah! Bread! *(He offers it.)*

QUEEN. Oh, thank you, sir. May you be rewarded for your gentle heart.

BLUE PRINCE. Thank you.

(He stands gazing at her. There is an awkward pause.)

QUEEN. A blessing on you, sir.

BLUE PRINCE. Thank you. *(He indicates the crust.)* Bread.

QUEEN. Ah, you have saved the life of a poor old woman…

BLUE PRINCE. Eat it.

QUEEN. *(Embarrassed.)* I—er—you—er…*(She takes a bite and mumbles something.)*

BLUE PRINCE. What?

QUEEN. *(Swallowing with great difficulty.)* I'm almost too happy to eat, sir. Leave a poor old woman alone with her happiness, and…

BLUE PRINCE. Not too happy. Too weak. Help you eat. *(He breaks off a piece and holds it to her mouth. With a great effort the QUEEN disposes of it.)* Good! Again! *(She does it again.)* Now! *(She swallows another piece.)* Last piece! *(She takes it in. He pats her kindly on the back, and she nearly chokes.)* Good. Better now?

QUEEN. *(Weakly.)* Much.

BLUE PRINCE. Good day.

QUEEN. *(With an effort.)* Good day, kind gentleman.

(He goes out. The KING is just coming from the cottage, when he returns suddenly. The KING slips back again.)

BLUE PRINCE. Small piece left over. *(He gives it to her. She looks hopelessly at him.)* Good-bye. *(He goes.)*

QUEEN. *(Throwing the piece down violently.)* Ugh! What a man!

KING. *(Coming out.)* Well, well, my dear, we have discovered the winner.

QUEEN. *(From the heart.)* Detestable person!

KING. The rest of the competition is of course more in the nature of a formality…

QUEEN. Thank goodness.

KING. However, I think that it will prevent unnecessary discussion afterwards if we….Take care, here is another one. *(He hurries back.)*

Plays for Children

(Enter the RED PRINCE.)

QUEEN. *(With not nearly so much conviction.)* Could you spare a crust of bread, sir, for a poor hungry old woman?

RED PRINCE. A crust of bread, madam? Certainly. As luck will have it, I have a crust on me. My last one, but—your need is greater than mine. Eat, I pray.

QUEEN. Th-thank you, sir.

RED PRINCE. Not at all. Come, eat. Let me have the pleasure of seeing you eating.

QUEEN. M-might I take it home with me, pretty gentleman?

RED PRINCE. *(Firmly.)* No, no. I must see you eating. Come! I will take no denial.

QUEEN. Th-thank you, sir. *(Hopefully.)* Won't you share it with me?

RED PRINCE. No, I insist on your having it all. I am in the mood to be generous. Oblige me by eating it now for I am in a hurry; yet I will not go until you have eaten. *(She does her best.)* You eat but slowly. *(Sternly.)* Did you deceive me when you said you were hungry?

QUEEN. N-no. I'm very hungry. *(She eats.)*

RED PRINCE. That's better. Now understand—however poor I am, I can always find a crust of bread for an old woman. Always! Remember this when next you are hungry. You spoke? *(She shakes her head and goes on eating.)* Finished?

QUEEN. *(With great difficulty.)* Yes, thank you, pretty gentleman.

RED PRINCE. There's a piece on the ground there that you dropped. *(She eats it in dumb agony.)* Finished?

QUEEN. *(Huskily.)* Yes, thank you, pretty gentleman.

RED PRINCE. Then I will leave you, madam. Good morning.

(He goes out. The QUEEN rises in fury. The KING is about to come out of the cottage, when the YELLOW PRINCE enters. The QUEEN sits down again and mumbles something. It is certainly not an appeal for bread, but the YELLOW PRINCE is not to be denied.)

YELLOW PRINCE. *(Gallantly.)* My poor woman, you are in distress. It pains me to see it, madam, it pains me terribly. Can it be that you are hungry? I thought so, I thought so. Give me the great pleasure, madam, of relieving your hunger. See *(holding up his finger)* my own poor meal. Take it! It is yours.

QUEEN. *(With difficulty.)* I am not hungry.

YELLOW PRINCE. Ah, madam, I see what it is. You do not wish to deprive me. You tell yourself, perchance, that it is not fitting that one in your station of life should partake of the meals of the highly born. You are not used, you say, to the food of Princes. Your rougher palate…

QUEEN. *(Hopefully.)* Did you say food of princes?

YELLOW PRINCE. Where was I, madam? You interrupted me. No matter—eat. *(She takes the scarf and unties the ribbon.)* Ah, now I remember. I was saying that your rougher palate…

QUEEN. *(Discovering the worst.)* No! No! Not bread!

YELLOW PRINCE. Bread, madam, the staff of life. Come, madam, will you not eat? *(She tries desperately.)* What can be more delightful than a crust of bread by the wayside?

(The QUEEN shrieks and falls back in a swoon. The KING rushes out to her.)

KING. *(To YELLOW PRINCE.)* Quick, quick, find the Princess.

YELLOW PRINCE. The Princess—find the Princess!

(He goes vaguely off and we shall not see him again. But the WOODCUTTER and the PRINCESS do not need to be found. They are here.)

WOODCUTTER. *(To PRINCESS.)* Go to her, but don't show that you know me.

(He goes into the cottage, and the PRINCESS hastens to her father.)

PRINCESS. Father!

KING. Ah, my dear, you're just in time. Your mother…

PRINCESS. My mother?

KING. Yes, yes. A little plan of mine—of hers—your poor mother. Dear, dear!

PRINCESS. But what's the matter?

KING. She is suffering from a surfeit of bread, and…

(The WOODCUTTER comes up with a flagon of wine.)

WOODCUTTER. Poor old woman! She has fainted from exhaustion. Let me give her some…

QUEEN. *(Shrieking.)* No, no, not bread! I will *not* have any more bread.

Plays for Children

WOODCUTTER. Drink this, my poor woman.

QUEEN. *(Opening her eyes.)* Did you say drink? *(She seizes the flagon and drinks.)*

PRINCESS. Oh, sir, you have saved my mother's life!

WOODCUTTER. Not at all.

KING. I thank you, my man, I thank you.

QUEEN. My deliverer! Tell me who you are!

PRINCESS. It is my mother, the Queen, who asks you.

WOODCUTTER. *(Amazed, as well he may be.)* The Queen!

KING. Yes, yes. Certainly, the Queen.

WOODCUTTE. *(Taking off his hat.)* Pardon, your Majesty. I am a woodcutter, who lives alone here, far away from courts.

QUEEN. Well, you've got more sense in your head than any of the Princes that *I've* seen lately. You'd better come to court.

PRINCESS. *(Shyly.)* You will be very welcome, sir.

QUEEN. And you'd better marry the Princess.

KING. Isn't that perhaps going a *little* too far, dear?

QUEEN. Well, you wanted kindness of heart in your son-in-law, and you've got it. And he's got common sense too. *(To WOODCUTTER.)* Tell me, what do you think of bread as—as a form of nourishment?

WOODCUTTER. *(Cautiously.)* One can have too much of it.

QUEEN. Exactly my view. *(To KING.)* There you are, you see.

KING. Well, if you insist. The great thing, of course, is that our darling child should be happy.

PRINCESS. I will do my best, father.

(She takes the WOODCUTTER'S hand.)

KING. Then the marriage will take place this evening. *(With a wave of his wand.)* Let the revels begin.

(They begin.)

End of Play

Plays for Children

THE KNAVE OF HEARTS

by Louise Saunders

Characters

The Manager
Blue Hose
Yellow Hose
1st Herald
2nd Herald
Pompdebile The Eighth, King Of Hearts *(Pronounced Pomp-Dibiley.)*
The Chancellor
The Knave of Hearts
Ursula
The Lady Violetta
Six Little Pages

The action of the play takes place in the kitchens of Pompdebile the Eighth, King of Hearts.

The MANAGER appears before the curtain in doublet and hose. He carries a cap with a long, red feather.

THE MANAGER. *(Bowing deeply.)* Ladies and gentlemen, you are about to hear the truth of an old legend that has persisted wrongly through the ages, the truth that, until now, has been hid behind the embroidered curtain of a rhyme, about the Knave of Hearts, who was no knave but a very hero indeed. The truth, you will agree with me, gentlemen and most honored ladies, is rare! It is only the quiet, unimpassioned things of nature that seem what they are. Clouds rolled in massy radiance against the blue, pines shadowed deep and darkly green, mirrored in still waters, the contemplative mystery of the hills — these things which exist, absorbed but in their own existence — these are the perfect chalices of truth. But we, gentlemen and thrice honored ladies, flounder about in a tangled net of prejudice, of intrigue. We are blinded by conventions, we are crushed by misunderstanding, we are distracted by violence, we are deceived by hypocrisy, until only too often villains receive the rewards of nobility and the truly great-hearted are suspected, distrusted, and maligned. And so, ladies and gentlemen, for the sake of justice and also, I dare to hope, for your approval, I have taken my puppets down from their dusty shelves. I have polished their faces, brushed their clothes, and strung them on wires, so that they may enact for you this history.

(He parts the curtains, revealing two PASTRY COOKS in flaring white caps and spotless aprons leaning over in stiff profile, their wooden spoons, three feet long, pointing rigidly to the ceiling. They are in one of the kitchens of Pompdebile the Eighth, King of Hearts. It is a pleasant kitchen, with a row of little dormer windows and a huge stove, adorned with the crest of Pompdebile — a heart rampant, on a gold shield.)

THE MANAGER. You see here, ladies and gentlemen, two pastry cooks belonging to the royal household of Pompdebile the Eighth Blue Hose and Yellow Hose, by name. At a signal from me they will spring to action, and as they have been made with astonishing cleverness, they will bear every semblance of life. Happily, however, you need have no fear that, should they please you, the exulting wine of your appreciation may go to their heads — their heads being but things of wire and wood; and happily, too, as they are but wood and wire, they will be spared the shame and humiliation that would otherwise be theirs should they fail to meet with your approval. The play, most honored ladies and gentlemen, will now begin.

(He claps his hands. Instantly the two PASTRY COOKS come to life. The MANAGER bows himself off the stage.)

BLUE HOSE. Is everything ready for this great event?

YELLOW HOSE. Everything. The fire blazing in the stove, the Pages, dressed in their best, waiting in the pantry with their various jars full of the finest butter, the sweetest sugar, the hottest pepper, the richest milk, the —

BLUE HOSE. Yes, yes, no doubt. *(Thoughtfully.)* It is a great responsibility, this that they have put on our shoulders.

YELLOW HOSE. Ah, yes. I have never felt more important.

BLUE HOSE. Nor I more uncomfortable.

YELLOW HOSE. Even on the day, or rather the night, when I awoke and found myself famous — I refer to the time when I laid before an astonished world my creation, "Humming birds' hearts soufflé, au vin blanc" — I did not feel more important. It is a pleasing sensation!

BLUE HOSE. I like it not at all. It makes me dizzy, this eminence on which they have placed us. The Lady Violetta is slim and fair. She does not, in my opinion, look like the kind of person who is capable of making good pastry. I have discovered through long experience that it is the heaviest women who make the lightest pastry, and vice versa. Well, then, suppose that she does not pass this examination — suppose that her pastry is lumpy, white like the skin of a boiled fowl.

YELLOW HOSE. Then, according to the law of the Kingdom of Hearts, we must condemn it, and the Lady Violetta cannot become the bride of Pompdebile. Back to her native land she will be sent, riding a mule.

BLUE HOSE. And she is so pretty, so exquisite! What a law! What an outrageous law!

YELLOW HOSE. Outrageous law! How dare you! There is nothing so necessary to the welfare of the nation as our art. Good cooks make good tempers, don't they? Must not the queen set an example for the other women to follow? Did not our fathers and our grandfathers before us judge the dishes of the previous queens of hearts?

BLUE HOSE. I wish I were mixing the rolls for tomorrow's breakfast.

YELLOW HOSE. Bah! You are fit for nothing else. The affairs of state are beyond you.

(Distant sound of trumpets.)

BLUE HOSE. *(Nervously.)* What's that?

YELLOW HOSE. The King is approaching! The ceremonies are about to commence!

BLUE HOSE. Is everything ready?

YELLOW HOSE. I told you that everything was ready. Stand still; you are as white as a stalk of celery.

BLUE HOSE. *(Counting on his fingers.)* Apples, lemons, peaches, jam — Jam! Did you forget jam?

YELLOW HOSE. Zounds, I did!

BLUE HOSE. *(Wailing.)* We are lost!

YELLOW HOSE. She may not call for it. Both stand very erect and make a desperate effort to appear calm.

Plays for Children

BLUE HOSE. *(Very nervous.)* Which door? Which door?

YELLOW HOSE. The big one, idiot. Be still!

> *(The sound of trumpets increases, and cries of "Make way for the King." Two HERALDS come in and stand on either side of the door. The KING of Hearts, followed by ladies and gentlemen of the court. POMPDEBILE is in full regalia, and very imposing indeed with his red robe bordered with ermine, his crown and sceptre. After him comes the CHANCELLOR, an old man with a short, white beard. The KING strides in a particularly kingly fashion, pointing his toes in the air at every step, toward his throne, and sits down. The KNAVE walks behind him slowly. He has a sharp, pale face.)*

POMPDEBILE. *(Impressively.)* Lords and ladies of the court, this is an important moment in the history of our reign. The Lady Violetta, whom you love and respect — that is, I mean to say, whom the ladies love and the lords — er — respect, is about to prove whether or not she be fitted to hold the exalted position of Queen of Hearts, according to the law, made a thousand years ago by Pompdebile the Great, and steadily followed ever since. She will prepare with her own delicate, white hands a dish of pastry. This will be judged by the two finest pastry cooks in the land. *(BLUE HOSE and YELLOW HOSE bow deeply.)* If their verdict be favorable, she shall ride through the streets of the city on a white palfrey, garlanded with flowers. She will be crowned, the populace will cheer her, and she will reign by our side, attending to the domestic affairs of the realm, while we give our time to weightier matters. This of course you all understand is a time of great anxiety for the Lady Violetta. She will appear worried— *(To CHANCELLOR.)* The palfrey is in readiness, we suppose.

CHANCELLOR. It is, Your Majesty.

POMPDEBILE. Garlanded with flowers?

CHANCELLOR. With roses, Your Majesty.

KNAVE. *(Bowing.)* The Lady Violetta prefers violets, Your Majesty.

POMPDEBILE. Let there be a few violets put in with the roses — er – – We are ready for the ceremony to commence. We confess to a slight nervousness unbecoming to one of our station. The Lady Violetta, though trying at times, we have found — er — shall we say — er — satisfying?

KNAVE. *(Bowing.)* Intoxicating, Your Majesty?

CHANCELLOR. *(Shortly.)* His Majesty means nothing of the sort.

POMPDEBILE. No, of course not — er — The mule — Is that — did you —?

CHANCELLOR. *(In a grieved tone.)* This is hardly necessary. Have I ever neglected or forgotten any of your commands, Your Majesty?

POMPDEBILE. You have, often. However, don't be insulted. It takes a great deal of our time and it is most uninteresting.

CHANCELLOR. *(Indignantly.)* I resign, Your Majesty.

POMPDEBILE. Your thirty-seventh resignation will be accepted tomorrow. Just now it is our wish to begin at once. The anxiety that no doubt gathered in the breast of each of the seven successive Pompdebiles before us seems to have concentrated in ours. Already the people are clamoring at the gates of the palace to know the decision. Begin. Let the Pages be summoned.

KNAVE. *(Bowing.)* Beg pardon, Your Majesty; before summoning the Pages, should not the Lady Violetta be here?

POMPDEBILE. She should, and is, we presume, on the other side of that door — waiting breathlessly.

(The KNAVE quietly opens the door and closes it.)

KNAVE. *(Bowing.)* She is not, Your Majesty, on the other side of that door waiting breathlessly. In fact, to speak plainly, she is not on the other side of that door at all.

POMPDEBILE. Can that be true? Where are her ladies?

KNAVE. They are all there, Your Majesty.

POMPDEBILE. Summon one of them. *(The KNAVE goes out, shutting the door. He returns, following URSULA, who, very much frightened, throws herself at the King's feet.)* Where is your mistress?

URSULA. She has gone, Your Majesty.

POMPDEBILE. Gone! Where has she gone?

URSULA. I do not know, Your Majesty. She was with us a while ago, waiting there, as you commanded.

POMPDEBILE. Yes, and then — speak.

URSULA. Then she started out and forbade us to go with her.

POMPDEBILE. The thought of possible divorce from us was more than she could bear. Did she say anything before she left?

URSULA. *(Trembling.)* Yes, Your Majesty.

Plays for Children

POMPDEBILE. What was it? She may have gone to self-destruction. What was it?

URSULA. She said —

POMPDEBILE. Speak, woman, speak.

URSULA. She said that Your Majesty —

POMPDEBILE. A farewell message! Go on.

URSULA. *(Gasping.)* That Your Majesty was "pokey" and that she didn't intend to stay there any longer.

POMPDEBILE. *(Roaring.)* Pokey!

URSULA. Yes, Your Majesty, and she bade me call her when you came, but we can't find her, Your Majesty.

(The PASTRY COOKS whisper. URSULA is in tears.)

CHANCELLOR. This should not be countenanced, Your Majesty. The word "pokey" cannot be found in the dictionary. It is the most flagrant disrespect to use a word that is not in the dictionary in connection with a king.

POMPDEBILE. We are quite aware of that, Chancellor, and although we may appear calm on the surface, inwardly we are swelling, swelling, with rage and indignation.

KNAVE. *(Looking out the window.)* I see the Lady Violetta in the garden. *(He goes to the door and holds it open, bowing.)* The Lady Violetta is at the door, Your Majesty.

(Enter the LADY VIOLETTA, her purple train over her arm. She has been running.)

VIOLETTA. Am I late? I just remembered and came as fast as I could. I bumped into a sentry and he fell down. I didn't. That's strange, isn't it? I suppose it's because he stands in one position so long he — Why, Pompy dear, what's the matter? Oh, oh! *(Walking closer.)* Your feelings are hurt!

POMPDEBILE. Don't call us Pompy. It doesn't seem to matter to you whether you are divorced or not.

VIOLETTA. *(Anxiously.)* Is that why your feelings are hurt?

POMPDEBILE. Our feelings are not hurt, not at all.

VIOLETTA. Oh, yes, they are, Pompdebile dear. I know, because they are connected with your eyebrows. When your feelings go down, up go your eyebrows, and when your feelings go up, they go down—always.

POMPDEBILE. *(Severely.)* Where have you been?

VIOLETTA. I, just now?

POMPDEBILE. Just now, when you should have been outside that door waiting breathlessly.

VIOLETTA. I was in the garden. Really, Pompy, you couldn't expect me to stay all day in that ridiculous pantry; and as for being breathless, it's quite impossible to be it unless one has been jumping or something.

POMPDEBILE. What were you doing in the garden?

VIOLETTA. *(Laughing.)* Oh, it was too funny. I must tell you. I found a goat there who had a beard just like the Chancellor's — really it was quite remarkable, the resemblance — in other ways too. I took him by the horns and I looked deep into his eyes, and I said, "Chancellor, if you try to influence Pompy—"

POMPDEBILE. *(Shouting.)* Don't call us Pompy.

VIOLETTA Excuse me, Pomp — *(Checking herself.)*

KNAVE. And yet I think I remember hearing of an emperor, a great emperor, named Pompey.

POMPDEBILE. We know him not. Begin at once; the people are clamoring at the gates. Bring the ingredients.

(The PASTRY COOKS open the door, and, single file, six little BOYS march in, bearing large jars labeled butter, salt, flour, pepper, cinnamon, and milk. The COOKS place a table and a large bowl and a pan in front of the LADY VIOLETTA and give her a spoon. The six little BOYS stand three on each side.)

VIOLETTA. Oh, what darling little ingredients. May I have an apron, please?

(URSULA puts a silk apron, embroidered with red hearts, on the LADY VIOLETTA.)

BLUE HOSE. We were unable to find a little boy to carry the pepper, My Lady. They all would sneeze in such a disturbing way.

VIOLETTA. This is a perfectly controlled little boy. He hasn't sneezed once.

YELLOW HOSE That, if it please Your Ladyship, is not a little boy.

Plays for Children

VIOLETTA. Oh! How nice! Perhaps she will help me.

CHANCELLOR. *(Severely.)* You are allowed no help, Lady Violetta.

VIOLETTA. Oh, Chancellor, how cruel of you. *(She takes up the spoon, bowing.)* Your Majesty, Lords and Ladies of the court, I propose to make—*(impressively)*—raspberry tarts.

BLUE HOSE. Heaven be kind to us!

YELLOW HOSE. *(Suddenly agitated.)* Your Majesty, I implore your forgiveness. There is no raspberry jam in the palace.

POMPDEBILE. What! Who is responsible for this carelessness?

BLUE HOSE. I gave the order to the grocer, but it didn't come. *(Aside.)* I knew something like this would happen. I knew it.

VIOLETTA. *(Untying her apron.)* Then, Pompdebile, I'm very sorry — we shall have to postpone it.

CHANCELLOR. If I may be allowed to suggest, Lady Violetta can prepare something else.

KNAVE. The law distinctly says that the Queen-elect has the privilege of choosing the dish which she prefers to prepare.

VIOLETTA. Dear Pompdebile, let's give it up. It's such a silly law! Why should a great splendid ruler like you follow it just because one of your ancestors, who wasn't half as nice as you are, or one bit wiser, said to do it? Dearest Pompdebile, please.

POMPDEBILE. We are inclined to think that there maybe something in what the Lady Violetta says.

CHANCELLOR. I can no longer remain silent. It is due to that brilliant law of Pompdebile the First, justly called the Great, that all members of our male sex are well fed, and, as a natural consequence, happy.

KNAVE. The happiness of a set of moles who never knew the sunlight.

POMPDEBILE. If we made an effort, we could think of a new law — just as wise. It only requires effort.

CHANCELLOR. But the constitution. We can't touch the constitution.

POMPDEBILE. *(Starting up.)* We shall destroy the constitution!

CHANCELLOR. The people are clamoring at the gates!

POMPDEBILE. Oh, I forgot them. No, it has been carried too far. We shall have to go on. Proceed.

VIOLETTA. Without the raspberry jam?

POMPDEBILE. *(To KNAVE.)* Go you, and procure some. I will give a hundred golden guineas for it.

(The little BOY who holds the cinnamon pot comes forward.)

BOY. Please, Your Majesty, I have some.

POMPDEBILE. You! Where?

BOY. In my pocket. If someone would please hold my cinnamon jar — I could get it. *(URSULA takes it. The BOY struggles with his pocket and finally, triumphantly, pulls out a small jar.)* There!

VIOLETTA. How clever of you! Do you always do that?

BOY. What — eat raspberry jam?

VIOLETTA. No, supply the exact article needed from your pocket.

BOY. I eat it for my lunch. Please give me the hundred guineas.

VIOLETTA. Oh, yes — Chancellor — if I may trouble you.

(Holding out her hand.)

CHANCELLOR. Your Majesty, this is an outrage! Are you going to allow this?

POMPDEBILE. *(Sadly.)* Yes, Chancellor. We have such an impulsive nature!

(The LADY VIOLETTA receives the money.)

VIOLETTA. Thank you. *(She gives it to the BOY.)* Now we are ready to begin. Milk, please. *(The BOY who holds the milk jar comes forward and kneels.)* I take some of this milk and beat it well.

YELLOW HOSE. *(In a whisper.)* Beat it — milk!

VIOLETTA. Then I put in two tablespoonfuls of salt; taking great care that it falls exactly in the middle of the bowl. *(To the little BOY.)* Thank you, dear. Now the flour, no, the pepper, and then — one pound of butter. I hope that it is good butter, or the whole thing will be quite spoiled.

BLUE HOSE. This is the most astonishing thing I have ever witnessed.

YELLOW HOSE. I don't understand it.

VIOLETTA. *(Stirring.)* I find that the butter is not very good. It makes a great difference. I shall have to use more pepper to counteract it. That's better. *(She pours in pepper. The BOY with the pepper pot sneezes violently.)* Oh, oh, dear! Lend him your handkerchief, Chancellor. Knave, will you? *(YELLOW HOSE silences the boy's sneezes with the*

Plays for Children

Knave's handkerchief.) I think that they are going to turn out very well. Aren't you glad, Chancellor? You shall have one if you will be glad and smile nicely — a little brown tart with raspberry jam in the middle. Now for a dash of vinegar.

COOKS. *(In horror.)* Vinegar! Great Goslings! Vinegar!

VIOLETTA. *(Stops stirring.)* Vinegar will make them crumbly. Do you like them crumbly, Pompdebile, darling? They are really for you, you know, since I am trying, by this example, to show all the wives how to please all the husbands.

POMPDEBILE. Remember that they are to go in the museum with the tests of the previous Queens.

VIOLETTA. *(Thoughtfully.)* Oh, yes, I had forgotten that. Under the circumstances, I shall omit the vinegar. We don't want them too crumbly. They would fall about and catch the dust so frightfully. The museum-keeper would never forgive me in years to come. Now I dip them by the spoonful on this pan; fill them with the nice little boy's raspberry jam — I'm sorry I have to use it all, but you may lick the spoon — put them in the oven, slam the door. Now, my Lord Pompy, the fire will do the rest.

(She curtsies before the KING.)

POMPDEBILE. It gave us great pleasure to see the ease with which you performed your task. You must have been practising for weeks. This relieves, somewhat, the anxiety under which we have been suffering and makes us think that we would enjoy a game of checkers once more. How long a time will it take for your creation to be thoroughly done, so that it may be tested?

VIOLETTA. *(Considering.)* About twenty minutes, Pompy.

POMPDEBILE. *(To HERALD.)* Inform the people. Come, we will retire. *(To KNAVE.)* Let no one enter until the Lady Violetta commands.

(All exit, left, except the KNAVE. He stands in deep thought, his chin in hand — then exits slowly, right. The room is empty. The cuckoo clock strikes. Presently both right and left doors open stealthily. Enter LADY VIOLETTA at one door, the KNAVE at the other, backward, looking down the passage. They turn suddenly and see each other.)

VIOLETTA. *(Tearfully.)* O Knave, I can't cook! Anything — anything at all, not even a baked potato.

KNAVE. So I rather concluded, My Lady, a few minutes ago.

VIOLETTA. *(Pleadingly.)* Don't you think it might just happen that they turned out all right? *(Whispering.)* Take them out of the oven. Let's look.

KNAVE. That's what I intended to do before you came in. It's possible that a miracle has occurred. He tries the door of the oven.

VIOLETTA. Look out; it's hot. Here, take my handkerchief.

KNAVE. The gods forbid, My Lady.

(He takes his hat, and, folding it, opens the door and brings out the pan, which he puts on the table softly.)

VIOLETTA. *(With a look of horror.)* How queer! They've melted or something. See, they are quite soft and runny. Do you think that they will be good for anything, Knave?

KNAVE. For paste, My Lady, perhaps.

VIOLETTA. Oh, dear. Isn't it dreadful!

KNAVE. It is.

VIOLETTA. *(Beginning to cry.)* I don't want to be banished, especially on a mule —

KNAVE. Don't cry, My Lady. It's very — upsetting.

VIOLETTA. I would make a delightful queen. The fêtes that I would give — under the starlight, with soft music stealing from the shadows, fêtes all perfume and deep mystery, where the young — like you and me, Knave — would find the glowing flowers of youth ready to be gathered in all their dewy freshness!

KNAVE. Ah!

VIOLETTA. Those stupid tarts! And wouldn't I make a pretty picture riding on the white palfrey, garlanded with flowers, followed by the cheers of the populace — Long live Queen Violetta, long live Queen Violetta! Those abominable tarts!

KNAVE. I'm afraid that Her Ladyship is vain.

VIOLETTA. I am indeed. Isn't it fortunate?

KNAVE. Fortunate?

VIOLETTA. Well, I mean it would be fortunate if I were going to be queen. They get so much flattery. The queens who don't adore it as I do must be bored to death. Poor things! I'm never so happy as when I am being flattered. It makes me feel all warm and purry. That is another reason why I feel sure I was made to be a queen.

KNAVE. *(Looking ruefully at the pan.)* You will never be queen, My Lady, unless we can think of something quickly, some plan —

VIOLETTA. Oh, yes, dear Knave, please think of a plan at once. Banished people, I suppose, have to comb their own hair, put on their shoes, and button themselves up the back. I have never performed these estimable and worthy tasks, Knave. I don't know how; I don't even know how to scent my bath. I haven't the least idea what makes it smell deliciously of violets. I only know that it always does smell deliciously of violets because I wish it that way. I should be miserable; save me, Knave, please.

KNAVE. My mind is unhappily a blank, Your Majesty.

VIOLETTA. It's very unjust. Indeed, it's unjust! No other queen in the world has to understand cooking; even the Queen of Spades doesn't. Why should the Queen of Hearts, of all people!

KNAVE. Perhaps it is because — I have heard a proverb: "The way to the heart is through the—"

VIOLETTA. *(Angrily, stamping her foot.)* Don't repeat that hateful proverb! Nothing can make me more angry. I feel like crying when I hear it, too. Now see, I'm crying. You made me.

KNAVE. Why does that proverb make you cry, My Lady?

VIOLETTA. Oh, because it is such a stupid proverb and so silly, because it's true in most cases, and because — I don't know why.

KNAVE. We are a set of moles here. One might also say that we are a set of mules. How can moles or mules either be expected to understand the point of view of a Bird of Paradise when she—

VIOLETTA. Bird of Paradise! Do you mean me?

KNAVE. *(Bowing.)* I do, My Lady, figuratively speaking.

VIOLETTA. *(Drying her eyes.)* How very pretty of you! Do you know, I think that you would make a splendid chancellor.

KNAVE. Her Ladyship is vain, as I remarked before.

VIOLETTA. *(Coldly.)* As I remarked before, how fortunate. Have you anything to suggest — a plan?

KNAVE. If only there were time my wife could teach you. Her figure is squat, round, her nose is clumsy, and her eyes stumble over it; but her cooking, ah — *(He blows a kiss.)* — it is a thing to dream about. She cooks as naturally as the angels sing. The delicate flavors of her concoctions float over the palate like the perfumes of a thousand

Plays for Children

flowers. True, her temper, it is anything but sweet — However, I am conceded by many to be the most happily married man in the kingdom.

VIOLETTA. *(Sadly.)* Yes. That's all they care about here. One may be, oh, so cheerful and kind and nice in every other way, but if one can't cook nobody loves one at all.

KNAVE. Beasts! My higher nature cries out at them for holding such views. Fools! Swine! But my lower nature whispers that perhaps after all they are not far from right, and as my lower nature is the only one that ever gets any encouragement—

VIOLETTA. Then you think that there is nothing to be done — I shall have to be banished?

KNAVE. I'm afraid — Wait, I have an idea! *(Excitedly.)* Dulcinea, my wife — her name is Dulcinea — made known to me this morning, very forcibly — Yes, I remember, I'm sure - Yes, she was going to bake this very morning some raspberry tarts — a dish in which she particularly excels — If I could only procure some of them and bring them here!

VIOLETTA. Oh, Knave, dearest, sweetest Knave, could you, I mean, would you? Is there time? The court will return. They tiptoe to the door and listen stealthily.

KNAVE. I shall run as fast as I can. Don't let anyone come in until I get back, if you can help it. He jumps on the table, ready to go out the window.

VIOLETTA. Oh, Knave, how clever of you to think of it. It is the custom for the King to grant a boon to the Queen at her coronation. I shall ask that you be made Chancellor.

KNAVE. *(Turning back.)* Oh, please don't, My Lady, I implore you.

VIOLETTA. Why not?

KNAVE. It would give me social position, My Lady, and that I would rather die than possess. Oh, how we argue about that, my wife and I! Dulcinea wishes to climb, and the higher she climbs, the less she cooks. Should you have me made Chancellor, she would never wield a spoon again.

VIOLETTA. *(Pursing her lips.)* But it doesn't seem fair, exactly. Think of how much I shall be indebted to her. If she enjoys social position, I might as well give her some. We have lots and lots of it lying around.

Plays for Children

KNAVE. She wouldn't, My Lady, she wouldn't enjoy it. Dulcinea is a true genius, you understand, and the happiness of a genius lies solely in using his gift. If she didn't cook she would be miserable, although she might not be aware of it, I'm perfectly sure.

VIOLETTA. Then I shall take all social position away from you. You shall rank below the scullery maids. Do you like that better? Hurry, please.

KNAVE. Thank you, My Lady; it will suit me perfectly.

(He goes out with the tarts. VIOLETTA listens anxiously for a minute; then she takes her skirt between the tips of her fingers and practises in pantomime her anticipated ride on the palfrey. She bows, smiles, kisses her hand, until suddenly she remembers the mule standing outside the gates of the palace. That thought saddens her, so she curls up in Pompdebile's throne and cries softly, wiping away her tears with a lace handkerchief. There is a knock. She flies to the door and holds it shut.)

VIOLETTA. *(Breathlessly.)* Who is there?

CHANCELLOR. It is I, Lady Violetta. The King wishes to return.

VIOLETTA. *(Alarmed.)* Return! Does he? But the tarts are not done. They are not done at all!

CHANCELLOR. You said they would be ready in twenty minutes. His Majesty is impatient.

VIOLETTA. Did you play a game of checkers with him, Chancellor?

CHANCELLOR. Yes.

VIOLETTA. And did you beat him?

CHANCELLOR. *(Shortly.)* I did not.

VIOLETTA. *(Laughing.)* How sweet of you! Would you mind doing it again just for me? Or would it be too great a strain on you to keep from beating him twice in succession?

CHANCELLOR. I shall tell the King that you refuse admission.

(VIOLETTA runs to the window to see if the KNAVE is in sight. The CHANCELLOR returns and knocks.)

CHANCELLOR. The King wishes to come in.

VIOLETTA. But the checkers!

CHANCELLOR. The Knights of the Checker Board have taken them away.

VIOLETTA. But the tarts aren't done, really.

Plays for Children

CHANCELLOR. You said twenty minutes.

VIOLETTA. No, I didn't — at least, I said twenty minutes for them to get good and warm and another twenty minutes for them to become brown. That makes forty — don't you remember?

CHANCELLOR. I shall carry your message to His Majesty.

VIOLETTA again runs to the window and peers anxiously up the road.

CHANCELLOR. *(Knocking loudly.)* The King commands you to open the door.

VIOLETTA. Commands! Tell him — Is he there — with you?

CHANCELLOR. His Majesty is at the door.

VIOLETTA. Pompy, I think you are rude, very rude indeed. I don't see how you can be so rude — to command me, your own Violetta who loves you so. *(She again looks in vain for the KNAVE.)* Oh, dear! *(Wringing her hands.)* Where can he be!

POMPDEBILE. *(Outside.)* This is nonsense. Don't you see how worried we are? It is a compliment to you —

VIOLETTA. Well, come in; I don't care — only I'm sure they are not finished.

(She opens the door for the KING, the CHANCELLOR, and the two PASTRY COOKS. The KING walks to his throne. He finds Lady Violetta's lace handkerchief on it.)

POMPDEBILE. *(Holding up handkerchief.)* What is this?

VIOLETTA. Oh, that's my handkerchief.

POMPDEBILE. It is very damp. Can it be that you are anxious, that you are afraid?

VIOLETTA. How Silly, Pompy. I washed my hands, as one always does after cooking; — *(To the PASTRY COOKS.)* — doesn't one? But there was no towel, so I used my handkerchief instead of my petticoat, which is made of chiffon and is very perishable.

CHANCELLOR. Is the Lady Violetta ready to produce her work?

VIOLETTA. I don't understand what you mean by work, Chancellor. Oh, the tarts! *(Nervously.)* They were quite simple — quite simple to make — no work at all — A little imagination is all one needs for such things, just imagination. You agree with me, don't you, Pompy, that imagination will work wonders — will do almost anything, in fact? I remember —

Plays for Children

POMPDEBILE. The Pastry Cooks will remove the tarts from the oven.

VIOLETTA. Oh, no, Pompy! They are not finished or cooked, or whatever one calls it. They are not. The last five minutes is of the greatest importance. Please don't let them touch them! Please —

POMPDEBILE. There, there, my dear Violetta, calm yourself. If you wish, they will put them back again. There can be no harm in looking at them. Come, I will hold your hand.

VIOLETTA. That will help a great deal, Pompy, your holding my hand.

(She scrambles up on the throne beside the KING.)

CHANCELLOR. *(In horror.)* On the throne, Your Majesty?

POMPDEBILE. Of course not, Chancellor. We regret that you are not yet entitled to sit on the throne, my dear. In a little while —

VIOLETTA. *(Coming down.)* Oh, I see. May I sit here, Chancellor, in this seemingly humble position at his feet? Of course, I can't really be humble when he is holding my hand and enjoying it so much.

POMPDEBILE. Violetta! *(To the PASTRY COOKS.)* Sample the tarts. This suspense is unbearable!

(The KING'S voice is husky with excitement. The two PASTRY COOKS, after bowing with great ceremony to the KING, to each other, to the CHANCELLOR — for this is the most important moment of their lives by far, — walk to the oven door and open it, impressively. They fall back in astonishment so great that they lose their balance, but they quickly scramble to their feet again.)

YELLOW HOSE. Your Majesty, there are no tarts there!

BLUE HOSE. Your Majesty, the tarts have gone!

VIOLETTA. *(Clasping her hands.)* Gone! Oh, where could they have gone?

POMPDEBILE. *(Coming down from throne.)* That is impossible.

PASTRY COOKS. *(Greatly excited.)* You see, you see, the oven is empty as a drum.

POMPDEBILE. *(To VIOLETTA.)* Did you go out of this room?

VIOLETTA. *(Wailing.)* Only for a few minutes, Pompy, to powder my nose before the mirror in the pantry. *(To PASTRY COOKS.)* When one cooks one becomes so disheveled, doesn't one? But if I had thought for one little minute —

POMPDEBILE. *(Interrupting.)* The tarts have been stolen!

VIOLETTA. *(With a shriek, throwing herself on a chair.)* Stolen! Oh, I shall faint; help me. Oh, oh, to think that any one would take my delicious little, my dear little tarts. My salts. Oh! Oh!

(PASTRY COOKS run to the door and call.)

YELLOW HOSE. Salts! Bring the Lady Violetta's salts.

BLUE HOSE. The Lady Violetta has fainted!

(URSULA enters hurriedly bearing a smelling-bottle.)

URSULA. Here, here — What has happened? Oh, My Lady, my sweet mistress!

POMPDEBILE. Some wretch has stolen the tarts.

(LADY VIOLETTA moans.)

URSULA. Bring some water. I will take off her headdress and bathe her forehead.

VIOLETTA. *(Sitting up.)* I feel better now. Where am I? What is the matter? I remember. Oh, my poor tarts! She buries her face in her hands.

CHANCELLOR. *(Suspiciously.)* Your Majesty, this is very strange.

URSULA. *(Excitedly.)* I know, Your Majesty. It was the Knave. One of the Queen's women, who was walking in the garden, saw the Knave jump out of this window with a tray in his hand. It was the Knave.

VIOLETTA. Oh, I don't think it was he. I don't, really.

POMPDEBILE. The scoundrel. Of course it was he. We shall banish him for this or have him beheaded.

CHANCELLOR. It should have been done long ago, Your Majesty.

POMPDEBILE. You are right.

CHANCELLOR. Your Majesty will never listen to me.

POMPDEBILE. We do listen to you. Be quiet.

VIOLETTA. What are you going to do, Pompy, dear?

POMPDEBILE. Herald, issue a proclamation at once. Let it be known all over the Kingdom that I desire that the Knave be brought here dead or alive. Send the royal detectives and policemen in every direction.

CHANCELLOR. Excellent; just what I should have advised had Your Majesty listened to me.

Plays for Children

POMPDEBILE. *(In a rage.)* Be quiet. *(Exit HERALD.)* I never have a brilliant thought but you claim it. It is insufferable!

(The HERALDS can be heard in the distance.)

CHANCELLOR. I resign.

POMPDEBILE. Good. We accept your thirty-eighth resignation at once.

CHANCELLOR. You did me the honor to appoint me as your Chancellor, Your Majesty, yet never, never do you give me an opportunity to chancel. That is my only grievance. You must admit, Your Majesty, that as your advisers advise you, as your dressers dress you, as your hunters hunt, as your bakers bake, your Chancellor should be allowed to chancel. However, I will be just — as I have been with you so long; before I leave you, I will give you a month's notice.

POMPDEBILE. That isn't necessary.

CHANCELLOR. *(Referring to the constitution hanging at his belt.)* It's in the constitution.

POMPDEBILE. Be quiet.

VIOLETTA. Well, I think as things have turned out so — so unfortunately, I shall change my gown. *(To URSULA.)* Put out my cloth of silver with the moonstones. It is always a relief to change one's gown. May I have my handkerchief, Pompy? Rather a pretty one, isn't it, Pompy? Of course you don't object to my calling you Pompy now. When I'm in trouble it's a comfort, like holding your hand.

POMPDEBILE. *(Magnanimously.)* You may hold our hand too, Violetta.

VIOLETTA. *(Fervently.)* Oh, how good you are, how sympathetic! But you see it's impossible just now, as I have to change my gown — unless you will come with me while I change.

CHANCELLOR. *(In a voice charged with inexpressible horror.)* Your Majesty!

POMPDEBILE. Be quiet! You have been discharged!

(He starts to descend, when a HERALD bursts through the door in a state of great excitement. He kneels before POMPDEBILE.)

HERALD. We have found him; we have found him, Your Majesty. In fact, I found him all by myself! He was sitting under the shrubbery eating a tart. I stumbled over one of his legs and fell. "How easy it is to send man and all his pride into the dust," he said, and then — I saw him!

POMPDEBILE. Eating a tart! Eating a tart, did you say? The scoundrel! Bring him here immediately.

(The HERALD rushes out and returns with the KNAVE, followed by the six little PAGES. The KNAVE carries a tray of tarts in his hand.)

POMPDEBILE. *(Almost speechless with rage.)* How dare you — you — you—

KNAVE. *(Bowing.)* Knave, Your Majesty.

POMPDEBILE. You Knave, you shall be punished for this.

CHANCELLOR. Behead him, Your Majesty.

POMPDEBILE. Yes, behead him at once.

VIOLETTA. Oh, no, Pompy, not that! It is not severe enough.

POMPDEBILE. Not severe enough, to cut off a man's head! Really, Violetta—

VIOLETTA. No, because, you see, when one has been beheaded, one's consciousness that one has been beheaded comes off too. It is inevitable. And then, what does it matter, when one doesn't know? Let us think of something really cruel — really fiendish. I have it — deprive him of social position for the rest of his life — force him to remain a mere knave, forever.

POMPDEBILE. You are right.

KNAVE. Terrible as this punishment is, I admit that I deserve it, Your Majesty.

POMPDEBILE. What prompted you to commit this dastardly crime?

KNAVE. All my life I have had a craving for tarts of any kind. There is something in my nature that demands tarts — something in my constitution that cries out for them — and I obey my constitution as rigidly as does the Chancellor seek to obey his. I was in the garden reading, as is my habit, when a delicate odor floated to my nostrils, a persuasive odor, a seductive, light brown, flaky odor, an odor so enticing, so suggestive of tarts fit for the gods that I could stand it no longer. It was stronger than I. With one gesture I threw reputation, my chances for future happiness, to the winds, and leaped through the window. The odor led me to the oven; I seized a tart, and, eating it, experienced the one perfect moment of my existence. After having eaten that one tart, my craving for other tarts has

Plays for Children

disappeared. I shall live with the memory of that first tart before me forever, or die content, having tasted true perfection.

POMPDEBILE. M-m-m, how extraordinary! Let him be beaten fifteen strokes on the back. Now, Pastry Cooks to the Royal Household, we await your decision!

(The COOKS bow as before, then each selects a tart from the tray on the table, lifts it high, then puts it in his mouth. An expression of absolute ecstasy and beatitude comes over their faces. They clasp hands, then fall on each other's necks, weeping.)

POMPDEBILE. *(Impatiently.)* What on earth is the matter?

YELLOW HOSE. Excuse our emotion. It is because we have at last encountered a true genius, a great master, or rather mistress, of our art.

(They bow to VIOLETTA.)

POMPDEBILE. They are good, then?

BLUE HOSE. *(His eyes to heaven.)* Good! They are angelic!

POMPDEBILE. Give one of the tarts to us. We would sample it.

(The PASTRY COOKS hand the tray to the KING, who selects a tart and eats it.)

POMPDEBILE. *(To VIOLETTA.)* My dear, they are marvels! marvels! *(He comes down from the throne and leads VIOLETTA up to the dais.)* Your throne, my dear.

VIOLETTA. *(Sitting down, with a sigh.)* I'm glad it's such a comfortable one.

POMPDEBILE. Knave, we forgive your offense. The temptation was very great. There are things that mere human nature cannot be expected to resist. Another tart, Cooks, and yet another!

CHANCELLOR. But, Your Majesty, don't eat them all. They must go to the museum with the dishes of the previous Queens of Hearts.

YELLOW HOSE. A museum — those tarts! As well lock a rose in a money-box!

CHANCELLOR. But the constitution commands it. How else can we commemorate, for future generations, this event?

KNAVE. An Your Majesty, please, I will commemorate it in a rhyme.

POMPDEBILE. How can a mere rhyme serve to keep this affair in the minds of the people?

KNAVE. It is the only way to keep it in the minds of the people. No event is truly deathless unless its monument be built in rhyme. Consider that fall which, though insignificant in itself, became the most famous of all history, because someone happened to put it into rhyme. The crash of it sounded through centuries and will vibrate for generations to come.

VIOLETTA. You mean the fall of the Holy Roman Empire?

KNAVE. No, Madam, I refer to the fall of Humpty Dumpty.

POMPDEBILE. Well, make your rhyme. In the meantime let us celebrate. You may all have one tart. *(The PASTRY COOKS pass the tarts. To VIOLETTA.)* Are you willing, dear, to ride the white palfrey garlanded with flowers through the streets of the city?

VIOLETTA. Willing! I have been practising for days!

POMPDEBILE. The people, I suppose, are still clamoring at the gates.

VIOLETTA. Oh, yes, they must clamor. I want them to. Herald, tell them that to every man I shall toss a flower, to every woman a shining gold piece, but to the babies I shall throw only kisses, thousands of them, like little winged birds. Kisses and gold and roses! They will surely love me then!

CHANCELLOR. Your Majesty, I protest. Of what possible use to the people—?

POMPDEBILE. Be quiet. The Queen may scatter what she pleases.

KNAVE. My rhyme is ready, Your Majesty.

POMPDEBILE. Repeat it.

KNAVE. The Queen of Hearts She made some tarts
All on a summer's day.
The Knave of Hearts
He stole those tarts
And took them quite away.
The King of Hearts
Called for those tarts
And beat the Knave full sore.
The Knave of Hearts
Brought back the tarts
And vowed he'd sin no more.

VIOLETTA. *(Earnestly.)* My dear Knave, how wonderful of you! You shall be Poet Laureate. A Poet Laureate has no social position, has he?

Plays for Children

KNAVE. It depends, Your Majesty, upon whether or not he chooses to be more laureate than poet.

VIOLETTA. *(Rising, her eyes closed in ecstasy.)* Your Majesty! Those words go to my head — like wine!

KNAVE. Long live Pompdebile the Eighth, and Queen Violetta!

(The trumpets sound.)

HERALDS. Make way for Pompdebile the Eighth, and Queen Vi-oletta!

VIOLETTA. *(Excitedly.)* Vee-oletta, please!

HERALDS. Make way for Pompdebile the Eighth, and Queen Vee-oletta—

(The KING and QUEEN show themselves at the door and the people can be heard clamoring outside.)

Curtain

End of Play

CINDERELLA

by Marguerite Merington

Characters

Goodman
Goodwife, who is not, however, a very good wife.
Ella, the Goodman's daughter by his first and good wife.
Vainbetty, Ella's step-sister
Scratchcatty, Ella's other step-sister
Dame Truly
Prince Affability
Royal Herald

Scene 1
The Goodman's cottage

Scene 2
Same. Three nights later

Scene 3
Same. The next morning

SCENE 1

The Goodman's cottage.

When the lights rise, the stage is empty. From outside the GOODWIFE enters, as usual in a bad temper. She looks about, then calls:

GOODWIFE. Cinderella! Where is that kitchen-wench? Crying over her mother's grave as usual, I'll be bound! *(Taking off bonnet and shawl.)*

Plays for Children

And I worn out with addressing a Mother's Aid Society gathering on how to bring up children! Really it is enough to provoke a saint! Cinderella! Cin- der-el-la!

ELLA. *(Coming from scullery.)* Here I am, Mother.

GOODWIFE. How often am I to tell you not to mother me, Miss?

ELLA. Pardon, Madam. I forgot.

GOODWIFE. Why isn't supper on the table? I told you sundown would see me back!

ELLA. I thought you would wait for my father to return from the fair, Madam.

GOODWIFE. Forget, please, that my husband happens to be your father, and remember only that I am mistress of this house. Serve the food and call my daughters.

(ELLA scurries to make dinner ready upon the table. VAINBETTY and SCRATCHCATTY, her step-sisters, are heard in their room, calling her.)

VAINBETTY. Cinderella! Here, lazybones, come and pin up my hair!

SCRATCHCATTY. Cinerella! Come, lace my bodice!

ELLA. Coming, sister Vainbett. In a minute, sister Scratchcatty.

THE TWO. Sister! Sis-ter? You kitchen-wench, you!

ELLA. Pardon, young ladies, I forgot.

GOODWIFE. Come, come, don't you see that I'm at table?

(VAINBETTY and SCRATCHCATTY enter and flop into their chairs at the table.)

SCRATCHCATTY. Here, lace me while I eat! *(ELLA obeys.)* Ouch, you're squeezing me to death, you vixen!

VAINBETTY. Put these hairpins in, and carefully! Ouch, you're tugging, you wild cat, you!

(With very bad table manners, they eat their dinner. ELLA rakes some food from the table, about to place it on hearth.)

GOODWIFE. *(Snatching this from her.)* What are you dong? Filching the pick of the food for your own greed?

ELLA. Madam indeed it's for my father when he returns. I meant no harm.

GOODWIFE. The trouble is, you haven't enough to do. Here. *(Takes shovelful of cinders from hearth, and empties them out the side window.)* Sift those cinders!

ELLA. Yes, Madam.

GOODWIFE. *(Returns to table.)* It's the last time I will marry a man with a daughter. As I said in my speech at the Mother's Aid Society, children should be brought up, and step-children should be taken down. How they applauded! But this one gives not the slightest excuse for discipline! It is an insult for a step-daughter to be as willing and obedient as this one!

VAINBETTY. She's tidy, too. Or she would be, if I didn't make slits with my scissors in her clothes!

SCRATCHCATTY. And she is so stupidly clean she keeps me busy smutting up her rags with ashes.

GOODWIFE. And good-looking! She would make you two look like caricatures if she were to suspect what a beauty she is! *(Sighs.)*

THE TWO. *(Alarmed.)* For mercy's sake don't let her suspect it!

(There is a knock at the door. All exclaim, 'Who's that?)

SCRATCHCATTY. It's old Dame Truly. I can hear her stick.

VAINBETTY. That old bore, with her sharp eyes and sharper tongue. Don't let her in!

GOODWIFE. Yes, yes; it won't do to offend her. For all she dresses so shabbily she is so independent in her speech she must have money.

(When the knock is repeated GOODWIFE opens the door.)

DAME TRULY. *(Hobbling in.)* Greetings on this household.

GOODWIFE. Dear Dame Truly. What a delightful surprise! Forgive our keeping you so long. We waited for our maid to open for you, but the stupid thing is never on hand when needed.

DAME TRULY. Ah, then you keep a maid?

GOODWIFE. Of course we do! Certainly we do! People in our position!

DAME TRULY. I ask and indeed that is why I have called because a rumor is abroad that your husband's daughter, Ella, bears all the brunt of the housework.

GOODWIFE. What! Darling little Ella! That precious child!

DAME TRULY. And, speaking of Ella, where is she?

Plays for Children

(ELLA advances from scullery.)

GOODWIFE. *(Hurriedly.)* Visiting her godmother. *(Waves ELLA back.)*

VAINBETTY. *(Almost at the same time, hurriedly.)* At boarding school!

SCRATCHCATTY. *(At the same time.)* Gone with her father to the fair!

DAME TRULY. Visiting her godmother, at boarding-school, and gone with her father to the fair! It must be hard to keep up with little Ella.

GOODWIFE. Ah, the young folks are great gadabouts, these days. Let me help you to potato-cake. And try the stirabout. Just a morsel. One, wee taste.

DAME TRULY. Mmm, delicious. Your maid is a good cook.

GOOD WIFE. That stupid thing? My daughters here are the accomplished ones!

DAME TRULY. Indeed! *(To VAIN BETTY.)* What's your recipe for potato-cake?

VAINBETTY. Why, you make a potato, and then a cake. I mean you take a potato and a cake and then you bake a potato and a cake, and and then you just go ahead!

DAME TRULY. Highly original. *(To SCRATCHCATTY.)* And stirabout?

SCRATCHCATTY. Why, you stir it about about the kitchen. I mean, about an hour or so. And then you keep on stirring it about until it is stirabout, you know.

DAME TRULY. Lucidity itself! That maid of yours, you do not find her satisfactory?

THE OTHERS. Satisfactory? If you only knew!

DAME TRULY. What wages do you pay her?

GOODWIFE. Wages? We give her a home, through charity!

DAME TRULY. Ah, then she meets with charity here. She finds this a home. And yet she has no claim on you?

GOODWIFE. None. Not the slightest

DAME TRULY. Then she is free to leave you. Then I can take her off your hands.

GOODWIFE. Wait, please. After all my kindness I have some claim on her.

DAME TRULY. Couldn't your claim be bought off?

GOODWIFE. *(Greedily.)* How much would you give?

DAME TRULY. I should have to ascertain her worth. Call her.

GOODWIFE. Cinderella!

(ELLA enters, and stands timidly before them.)

DAME TRULY. Strange, she looks like someone I used to know; the daughter of an old schoolmate.

VAINBETTY. Many people look like other people. I've often noticed it.

DAME TRULY. Pity that charity can't find her a whole frock, a pretty hair-ribbon.

SCRATCHCATTY. Wasted on her. She slits and smutties everything!

GOODWIFE. We do our best, my girls and I, but the wench is stupidity itself!

DAME TRULY. Odd, but I never yet have come across a stupid child. Stupid parents, guardians, and employers, often. But a stupid child means a child set to a task for which it is not fitted. Let me take this one off your hands

GOODWIFE. Oh, if the ingrate wants to go, after all my kindness to her!

DAME TRULY. Child, answer fearlessly. Are you happy here?

(ELLA is silent.)

GOODWIFE. Tell the lady you are happy as can be, or you'll know what's good for you!

DAME TRULY. *(To ELLA.)* This is not a prison. Since no ties bind you, the door stands open. And in my heart I promise you a home. Well, will you come?

ELLA. Dame, I thank you, but I cannot.

DAME TRULY. Cannot? 'Tis but the act of crossing the threshold. Try.

ELLA. Madam, I thank you, but I may not

DAME TRULY. Will not? How is that?

ELLA. I promised my dear departed mother that I would take care of my father. I cannot leave him

GOODWIFE. *(Triumphant.)* Well, Dame, are you answered?

DAME TRULY. I am answered. *(Turns and hobbles out.)* Good day to you all.

Plays for Children

GOODWIFE. That was an escape! The old meddler, I doubt if she has a penny, for all her overbearing ways. Here, you, Cinderella, you; come and clear the table.

(*ELLA clears the table. Her father, GOODMAN, enters laden with bundles.*)

GOODMAN. Good evening

ELLA. *(Runs to greet him.)* Father! Welcome home! Are you tired and hungry, Father?

GOODWIFE. *(Interposing.)* Get you gone about your business, kitchen-wench!

GOODMAN. Come, now, my good Peppercornelia!

GOODWIFE. Don't you Peppercornelia me. Where are the new clothes you promised me and my daughters?

VAINBETTY and **SCRATCHCATTY**. Yes, where are our new clothes?

GOODWIFE. That satin gown, and head-dress with feathers. Where are they?

VAINBETTY and **SCRATCHCATTY**. Our silken frocks, dancing shoes with buckles, scarves, fans, wreaths, gloves and ornaments, where are they?

GOODMAN. *(Setting down bundles.)* All in good time. Service before silks and satins. I laid in a stock of household utensils! *(The women exclaim, disgusted.)* Here's a new kind of knife peels potatoes while you look at them. It says so, in the advertisement. *(Displays articles while describing them.)* Babies cry for it.

GOODWIFE. *(Dashing it from his hand.)* Simpleton.

GOODMAN. And here's a new invention. Read the prospectus! "It makes cinder-sifting a drawing-room accomplishment for the fairest of ladies! No happiness in the home without it!" We need it!

GOODWIFE. Give it to your ash-girl Cinderella! *(Throws it at ELLA.)* Where are our new clothes?

VAINBETTY and **SCRATCHCATTY**. Where are our new clothes?

GOODMAN. Here's a good investment. A sack of beans! A special brand, the merchant called them. Has-beens

GOODWIFE. Beans, beans! Fool! Where are our new clothes?

GOODMAN. Here's a bargain! A prize pumpkin! Such pies as you'll get out of it! The farmer that sold it to me as a favor told me that it's the best pumpkin on record! What do you say to that!

ELLA. Father! Oh, you dear Father!

GOODWIFE. *(Infuriated.)* Nincompoop! What sort of a figure shall I cut at Mother's Aid Society with a potato-knife? Answer me that! Can my Vainbetty go walking clothed in a cinder-sifter, or Scratchcatty attend parties in a sack of beans? As for your silly pumpkin —

(She dashes the pumpkin to the ground, and kicks it about, her daughters joining in the sport.)

GOODMAN. *(Trying to stop them.)* Wife! Peppercornelia! Young women, stop! Well, now, isn't it lucky it is such a tough one, else it never would have withstood such treatment.

GOODWIFE. *(Sinks into chair, exhausted.)* How come I to be married to such an insect!

GOODMAN. Come, now; this may cheer you up! *(Tosses a bundle into her lap.)* And you, too, young women; here's your finery! *(Gives them bundles.)* Silly fripperies, to my mind, and far beyond my means, but anything for a quiet life.

GOODWIFE. At last!

(She and her daughters undo the packages, with exclamations of satisfaction, taking out the finery these contain, displaying it, and adorning themselves with it.)

ELLA. *(Brings food and sets this before the GOODMAN.)* Here, Father. You must be hungry.

GOODMAN. Perhaps I am. I noticed an odd sensation inside me, and— *(Eats.)* Yes, it was hunger. Have you had your supper, Ella?

GOODWIFE. Oh, be sure she nibbled the choicest morsels while preparing the food.

ELLA. *(Going over to her step-sisters and looks at their finery.)* May I look? Oh, how pretty!

SCRATCHCATTY. Keep your smutty hands off my things, Miss!

GOODMAN. Here, little one; it's your turn now. You bade me bring you something.

GOODWIFE. *(Sharply.)* Don't tell me you spent money on *her*?

GOODMAN. She asked for nothing costing money.

Plays for Children

ELLA. Only the first bough that should brush your hat as you started homeward.

VAINBETTY. Just like her, the daffy thing!

GOODMAN. A child's innocent whim. And here it is, dear one.

(He gives ELLA a hazel bough.)

ELLA. *(Greatly pleased.)* Oh, Father, that is all I cared, that you should remember. Because lately you have seemed — forgive me, to forget.

GOODMAN. *(In undertone.)* For your own sake! Sh! *(Kisses her.)*

GOODWIFE. What's all that whispering about? Complaining of me and my daughters, I'll be bound.

SCRATCHCATTY. As usual. The cry-baby.

GOODMAN. The lass never complains, no matter what the provocation.

GOODWIFE. Oh, then she has provocation, you think? She says that I ill-treat her? *(She approaches ELLA menacingly.)* I'll teach you to carry tales, Miss.

VAINBETTY. Little tattle-tale!

GOODMAN. *(Protesting.)* Peppercornelia, the maid never has been used to harshness.

GOODWIFE. Tis time she should taste a dose. You're far too soft with her.

SCRATCHCATTY. I should say so. She's the worst spoiled child a perfect enfant terrible!

GOODWIFE. Bring me that hazel switch.

GOODMAN. You shall not lift a hand against her. Go outside, Ella.

(ELLA obeys.)

GOODWIFE. *(Infuriated.)* You defy me, do you? In my own house, too. Aye, my house. You forget, no doubt, that I made you sign it over to me. *(Calls and claps her hands.)* Cinderella! I want you.

VAINBETTY and **SCRATCHCATTY**. Come, Cinderella! We want you.

GOODWIFE. And bring that delicate little hazel bough! *(ELLA enters, with the bough.)* Give it to me! (ELLA obeys, and it is now seen that the bough has mysteriously grown.) What's this? I want the bough your father brought you.

ELLA. Madam, this is the same.

Plays for Children

GOODWIFE. The same? Tell the truth, Miss.

ELLA. Madam, that is the truth.

GOODWIFE. See what a paragon your child is!

GOODMAN. *(Snatching the switch.)* Hold! Where did you get this, Ella?

ELLA. Tis the same you brought me, sir.

GOODMAN. My dear, this is half as long. How can it be the same, my child?

GOODWIFE. *(Sneering.)* Aye, how can it be the same, my child?

ELLA. *(Taking the bough from her father.)* Father, I called on my mother's name, and I cried, and as my tears fell on the bough it grew, and grew, and…Oh, Father!

(She runs outside again, sobbing.)

GOODWIFE. Well, now are your eyes opened?

GOODMAN. I don't know what to think.

GOODWIFE. Don't exert your pin-head brains. I do the thinking for this family. Innocent little Ella. Artless maid. By cutting a longer, stouter bough she shrewdly planned to put herself beyond the power of my arm.

GOODMAN. Do you realize that no hazel tree grows within a mile of this spot? I know every growth hereabouts, and I tell you —

GOODWIFE. And I tell you I won't be tricked, laughed at to my face!

GOODMAN. I never yet have caught the lass in an untruth.

GOODWIFE. You, you blind mole. Anyone could take you in!

GOODMAN. Tis a fact I'm a bit credulous. Even I believed you when you swore you loved my child as your own, and would make a happy home for her and me!

GOODWIFE. That's right. Insult me, do!

VAINBETTY. I trust this sweet domestic scene draws near its conclusion. My sister and I are expecting company.

GOODMAN. I think I'll go brush up a bit! *(Exits.)*

VAINBETTY. Can't you send her away, get rid of her somehow; take her for a picnic and lose her in the forest

GOODWIFE. Can you dress your own hair?

SCRATCHCATTY. Can't you afford to pay a maid-servant?

Plays for Children

GOODWIFE. What hireling could get through the household drudgery that she does, and still have time to lace your bodice, eh? *(Walks to the window.)* The whole situation is uncanny. It gives me the creeps. Look yonder now. She's planted that sapling. Look! Look! As I watch, it is developing into a full-sized tree. Now it bears nuts. And now birds and squirrels are nesting in its branches!

VAINBETTY. That's easily explained. It is intensive farming. I learned about it at boarding-school.

SCRATCHCATTY. Or auto-hypnosis. Self-delusion. *(Whispers to her sister.)* In this case mother is flighty, not to say plain nutty! *(She and her sister laugh.)*

VAINBETTY. All the same we ought to get rid of her. She grows better looking every day! Whenever I look at her I want to seize her by the hair of her head, and — what business has a step-sister with such hair!

GOODWIFE. The trouble is, she is protected. Listen. She has a godmother.

SCRATCHCATTY. A godmother?

GOODWIFE. Ella's godmother is a very grand old lady, living in a castle. She has money!

VAINBETTY. Which she will leave to Ella. All the more reason for getting rid of Ella!

GOODWIFE. More easily said than done, since fairy godmothers have organized this Child Welfare movement. In the good old days nothing was simpler than to get rid of one's superfluous relations. One merely dropped them into the well, or took them to the circus and fed them to the bears, like buns! But, nowadays, the Health Inspectors, nosey creatures, analyze the well-water, for the relation-microbe, while as for the bears, they're so stupidly hygienic they won't look at anything but breakfast food! It's an outrage!

(A trumpet call is heard. All exclaim and run to the window.)

GOODMAN. *(Hurries in, in shirt-sleeves, putting coat on.)* What's this? A King's Herald here!

(There is a knock at the door.)

HERALD. *(Outside.)* Open, in the King's name! *(The GOODMAN opens. HERALD enters.)* In the name of King Pomposity the Twenty-Seventh! *(All bow.)* Hearken to the royal will. *(All bow again.)* I address the goodman, the goodwife, and the maidens of this household, greetings!

GOODWIFE. You see us before you.

HERALD. All?

GOODWIFE. All.

HERALD. Not so, according to the latest census. *(Opens a birch-bark scroll.)* There remains one Ella.

GOODWIFE. Oh, to be sure, our dear little Ella!

HERALD. Summon her, this dear little missing miss, Ella.

GOODWIFE. *(Claps hands, calls.)* Cinderella! Where has the little sunbeam flitted to! *(ELLA enters.)* Ah, here she is.

HERALD. *(Prepares to read from a parchment scroll.)* Good. "In the name of…" Hm, hm. "Whereas…" *(Clears throat.)* "Whereas His Royal Highness, the Prince Affability, has come of age…"

VAINBETTY. That dear Prince Affability.

SCRATCHCATTY. How gracious of him to have come of age.

HERALD. "And whereas 'tis meet that he should choose a bride…"

GOODWIFE, VAINBETTY and **SCRATCHCATTY** *(Nudge one another.)* A bride! The Prince would choose a bride!

HERALD. "His Majesty the King is graciously pleased to give a ball— *(ALL exclaim, "A ball!")*—at the royal palace, tonight, tomorrow night, and the night of the day after tomorrow, to which all families with marriageable daughters are bidden!" God save the King!

ALL. Long live the King!

(The HERALD goes. General excitement reigns. The GOODWIFE and her daughters bustle about, making preparations.)

VAINBETTY. A ball, three nights running, Cinderella, come pin these ornaments in my hair! The Prince, the Prince! A Prince's bride!

SCRATCHCATTY. Cinderella, come lace me tighter! A Prince's bride!

VAINBETTY. What is that I hear? Sister-in-law to royalty is as near as you may hope to get!

SCRATCHCATTY. Sister-in-law, yourself. And not even invited to a Sunday dinner, if you presume on the relationship!

VAINBETTY. Hear her! Hear her! I am the handsomer by far. Eh, Mother?

Plays for Children

SCRATCHCATTY. Just listen to her! Listen to her! My manner is incomparably the more taking! Eh, Mother?

GOODWIFE. Mother-in-law to a Prince. A near-queen-dowager, so to speak! The sentry will present arms, as I go and come! Don't waste breath disputing, daughters; 'twill mottle your complexions, make your noses red. Perhaps the Prince will pass a law enabling him to marry you both. My fan, get me my fan, you Cinderella, you! Lucky we have our new finery! Mother-in-law to a Prince! *(Parading up and down, making court curtseys.)*

VAINBETTY. *(Parading, as a queen.)* Princess Vainbetty. Future queen! Kiss my hand, varlet!

SCRATCHCATTY. *(Doing likewise.)* Scratchcatty, bride of His Royal Highness, Prince Affability. Daughter-in-law of King Pomposity the Twenty-Seventh. Queen Scratchcatty to be! Rise up, Sir Knight! Ladies, my train! My scepter, my crown! Bring me my scepter, crown!

GOODMAN. Well, upon my word! *(Roars with laughter.)* Tis like play acting. I vow I haven't laughed so much since the mummers passed this way!

GOODWIFE. *(Transfixing him with a haughty stare.)* Low lived caitiff! Can you deny that you are a low-lived caitiff?

GOODMAN. First let me look up "caitiff" in the dictionary.

GOODWIFE. You had better go harness your old horse to your old coach, and prepare to drive us to the ball!

GOODMAN. *(About to comply.)* Anything for a quiet life. Why don't you get ready, Ella?

GOODWIFE. Ella get ready for the ball?

ELLA. *(Overjoyed.)* Oh, Father, then I may accompany you?

GOODMAN. Why not? You are invited.

GOODWIFE. I have something to say about that. Her tasks are not yet done.

ELLA. *(Looks about, surprised.)* Madam, what remains?

GOODWIFE. What remains? Why, this!

(She seizes sack of beans and empties this out of window.)

GOODMAN. What are you doing? Emptying those fine old has-beens on to the ash-heap!

GOODWIFE. Precisely. Now you Cinderella, you. Sort those beans from the ashes, and you shall accompany me and my daughters to the ball.

(She throws sack to ELLA, the two daughters deriding her, meanwhile.)

GOODMAN. It's an outrage. But, never mind, lass, father will help you. Aye, with my new, patent cindersifter!

GOODWIFE. *(Interposing.)* You'll do nothing of the sort. You'll harness up the horses. But first you'll put on your Sunday coat *(Pushes him toward his room.)* I'm mistress in this house! *(ELLA signs to her father not to mind, and goes out quietly through the scullery. He also exits.)* That will cook her goose!

VAINBETTY. *(To her mother.)* Is my color high enough, or do I need another coat of paint? Have I shaped my eyebrows archly? *(Sweeping about the room.)* Do I manage my train right?

ELLA. *(Comes, by way of the scullery with the sack filled again.)* Here, Madam, are the beans. *(She places the sack on the table.)*

GOODWIFE. What's that? Already? Impossible!

(Her DAUGHTERS echo her surprise.)

GOODMAN. *(Coming from his room, neckcloth in hand.)* Ella, El-la! Here, child; come fold my neckcloth. No one does it so well

ELLA. *(Obeying him.)* There! No one will have a handsomer father at the ball.

GOODMAN. *(Sighing.)* Little one, my heart is heavy, leaving you behind.

ELLA. But I can go with you. I have finished my task.

GOODMAN. What? All ready?

ELLA. My doves and pigeons helped me, the darlings.

GOODMAN. Haste, then, and make ready, before the goodwife can change her mind.

VAINBETTY. What's all this? The kitchen-wench wishes to accompany us? First let her complete her task! *(She empties the sack out of window, as her mother did before.)* Let her sort the beans from the ashes, on my account.

GOODMAN. Tis an outrage. Why, one would think you had a grudge against the lass!

GOODWIFE. Stop your prating, and don court costume, good, my Lord, then haste to see wherefore the servitors delay the equipage!

Plays for Children

(The GOODMAN shakes his head, returns to his room. ELLA quietly takes the sack and goes out again. A knock is heard.)

SCRATCHCATTY. *(To her mother.)* Is my expression right? Delicate and languishing? Am I irresistible? *(Sweeping about.)* Do I manage *my* train right? *(Curtseys to an imaginary person.)* Your Royal Highness.

ELLA. *(Enters, with the sack filled.)* Here are the beans, all sorted out. My pigeons and doves helped me, the darlings!

GOODMAN. *(Coming from his room, fully dressed.)* Then make ready, child!

SCRATCHCATTY. Not so fast! Let her fill the sack again on my account! *(She also empties the sack out of window.)* Scullery-maid! You Cinderella, you!

GOODMAN. Now I protest, that's scandalous. But, this time, go she shall!

GOODWIFE. *(Pushing him toward the door.)* Cease prating, I say, and go order our equipage, summon our liveries!

(Wearily, the GOODMAN takes a lantern, and goes out. ELLA goes quietly through the scullery. The three women don their wraps.)

VAINBETTY. *(Looks out of side-window.)* 'Tis true, her doves and pigeons are helping her.

GOODWIFE. Well, what of that?

VAINBETTY. What if her father insists on taking her with us?

GOODWIFE. She has nothing fit to wear.

SCRATCHCATTY. She has her mother's clothes. Dainty, delicate; nothing that we couldn't get into!

GOODWIFE. That's true! *(She unlocks and opens the clothespress.)* What shall we do? Wait! I have it! *(She goes to the hearth, takes a shovelful of ashes, which she showers over the garments. Her DAUGHTERS, laughing fiendishly, assist her.)* There! And there. And there! Look out. I hear her coming.

ELLA. *(Enters, the sack filled.)* Here, Madam, are the beans.

GOODMAN. *(Appears at the door, whip in hand.)* Coach is ready! Well, my lass. How now?

ELLA. 'Tis done, Father. My doves and pigeons helped me, the darlings. And now really I may go to the ball, mayn't I?

GOODMAN. You may, and you shall. Or no one goes from this house tonight. Let that be understood! *(Makes a cut with the whip.)*

Plays for Children

GOODWIFE. Why threaten? No one prevents her. My daughters and I wait for her.

VAINBETTY. Surely we do.

SCRATCHCATTY. We'll even help her.

ELLA. *(Surprised and pleased.)* How kind! Madam, may I have your key to the clothes-press? My mother's clothes fit me as had they been fashioned for me.

GOODWIFE. Surely! I'll even unlock it for you, myself. *(She does so.)*

GOODMAN. Now this is as it should be! Motherly, sisterly, kind!

ELLA. I will not keep you long.

(She is about to take out a gown, cries out, horrified.)

GOODWIFE. *(With pretended sympathy.)* Why, what is the matter

GOODMAN. What ails you, lass?

ELLA. They are ruined, covered with ashes, soot my mother's dainty frocks!

GOODMAN. What devil's trick is this?

GOODWIFE. *(Bursting into mocking laughter.)* Ha, ha! Queen of the ash-heap! You'd go to the ball, would you? Cinderella at the ball!

VAINBETTY. Cendrillon, the kitchen-wench! Ha, ha, ha! Thought you'd dance with the Prince, no doubt!

SCRATCHCATTY. Come just as you are, in your sooty rags! You'd be the belle, I warrant! The Prince would fall in love with you, perhaps; aye, marry you!

(Mocking her with laughter, gibe, and fingers pointed at her, the three women go out. The GOODMAN follows, raising his hands in despair, as if to say that the situation is beyond him. The coach is heard, departing. ELLA who has stood confronting her tormenters with bowed head, cries softly. DAME TRULY enters unbeknownst to ELLA.)

ELLA. Oh, my mother! Oh, if only there were someone on earth to turn to!

DAME TRULY. There always is someone!

ELLA. Dame Truly! I did not know you were here.

DAME TRULY. I tell you, there always is someone. What about that fairy godmother of yours?

ELLA. Oh, she lives a long, long way away.

Plays for Children

DAME TRULY. Thoughts can travel long, long distances.

ELLA. She lives in a castle. My thoughts might not gain admittance there.

(A slight pause, during which both gaze into the embers.)

DAME TRULY. It's a pretty sight, the glow of the embers, isn't it?

ELLA. If I look hard enough, I can see the palace. And the ball! Oh, do you see it, too? The lights and the flowers, and the fountains. And do you hear the music? Oh, the music! It fairly makes one dance.

DAME TRULY. And the courtiers, the guests; the bowing and the bending, and all the silly flummery!

ELLA. The Prince, now I see the Prince.

DAME TRULY. Nice boy, the Prince. Good, clean boy. Well-brought up. Doesn't spend beyond his allowance. No borrowing. No gambling debts. A hard worker, too. Will make a good king, when his time comes.

ELLA. He's choosing a partner to tread a measure with him. It looks like it is, Vainbetty! How proudly my step-mother bears herself! And now he gives his hand to another lady. This time it is Scratchcatty. In a room far beyond I see my father, with other gentlemen, playing cards, and yawning. Poor father, he is not enjoying himself. But, oh, how beautiful it is, as they dance! And now, alas! The dream fades!

DAME TRULY. Those dreams are a short-lived. Very few of them get anywhere.

ELLA. But they give such pleasure, while they last; at least, all mine do.

DAME TRULY. That comes of having a good digestion. And so when I came in you were crying your eyes out, because you want to go to that ball. Well, why don't you go?

ELLA. Clothes. I have none befitting.

DAME TRULY. Your mother's.

ELLA. I don't know how I can explain, but cinders, ashes, soot!

DAME TRULY. Poof! Such things never hurt a really good material. A simple application of dew mixed with moonshine will renew them. Try it.

ELLA. *(Taking one of the flocks out.)* That sounds wonderful! Moonshine mixed with dew.

DAME TRULY. Go into the next room, and put on the dress.

ELLA. But —

DAME TRULY. Never mind, dear, just do it.

> (ELLA *exits with the dress. Left alone,* DAME TRULE *dances to the sound of elfish music, singing.*)

DAME TRULY. "Though not so young as I used to be,

> I'm blithe and nimble, as still you see.

> The years drop off, at an old refrain,

> And my heels are as young as my heart, again!"

ELLA. *(Enters, fastening the dress on.)* It is wonderful! It is far lovelier than before! See!

DAME TRULY. Not bad. Now you need a scarf.

ELLA. I fear I have none.

DAME TRULY. Luckily, I noticed one hanging on the tree as I came in. *(Points out window.)* The finest gossamer.

ELLA. Dear Dame, that is a cobweb!

DAME TRULY. Cobweb? Poof! What are young people's eyes good for, nowadays? A famous spinner has been at work on it for you. I notice they hung it, for safety, and also perhaps as an advertisement, on the tree. Bid your birds throw it down.

ELLA. I will! Little bird, little bird, on the tree, my gossamer scarf throw down to me!

> *(The sound of the birds answering is heard, as a beautiful scarf is thrown to her. She catches it through the window.)*

DAME TRULY. You see? So far so good. But you can't dance, in those old shoes.

ELLA. I have none others.

DAME TRULY. Dancing shoes, bronze-gold, satin-lined, and edged with fur, the tree-cobblers have been busy fabricating them in time! Look and see.

ELLA. *(Looks out of window.)* All I see are nuts upon the bough.

DAME TRULY. Nuts? Dancing-slippers. Ask for them.

ELLA. Little bird, little bird on the tree, my dancing-slippers throw down to me! *(Again the birds respond, and a pair of beautiful slippers is thrown to her. She exclaims with delight, and puts them on.)* Aren't they beautiful? They make my feet dance! Now at last I'm ready. *(Turns about for inspection.)* Is all as it should be, now?

Plays for Children

DAME TRULY. Yes, my dear, all is as it should be.

ELLA. Oh, I forgot. It is of no use. How can I go, without a coach to carry me?

DAME TRULY. Coach? Poof! There's one, under the table. *(Points with her stick)*

ELLA. That? Dear Dame, believe me, that is a pumpkin, not a coach

DAME TRULY. *(Emphasizing with her stick.)* A coach! Open the door while I roll it outside.

(ELLA obeys and DAME TRULY pushes the pumpkin out.)

ELLA. Why, even as I look at it, it is turning into the most beautiful gold coach! But horses, Dame, what shall I do for horses?

DAME TRULY. I saw six cream-white steeds out there. Look for yourself.

ELLA. *(Looks forth.)* I only see the field-mice, scuttling from their hiding-places.

DAME TRULY. Where are those grasshoppers? I mean, grooms.

(She strikes her stick upon the floor. The sound of champing horses is heard.)

ELLA. *(Looking from the window.)* It is as you say: six cream-white steeds! But who will drive me?

DAME TRULY. Your coachman. Hear him now, as usual, scolding the lackeys.

ELLA. *(Listens.)* Indeed, dear Dame, that is but the squirrels chattering.

DAME TRULY. Poof! Now look. See, the coachman? The coach awaits the Lady Ella's pleasure! Now, my child, go, enjoy yourself. But mind you leave the ball before the stroke of twelve. At midnight your finery will vanish, clothes and equipage, and you will become the little kitchen-wench again, the mock of the beholders, spurned by your stepmother and stepsisters, shaming your good father who is powerless to help you, discrediting your mother's memory.

ELLA. I will not forget. From my heart I thank you. *(Kisses DAME TRULY'S hand.)* I know you now. You are my fairy godmother!

DAME TRULY. Poof! Now go!

(ELLA runs towards the door, turns back around and waves one last time to DAME TRULE, and then runs off. The coach is heard departing, and the scene is veiled in darkness.)

Plays for Children

SCENE 2

Music is heard. In a mist, the PRINCE is dancing with ELLA, who is enjoying herself immensely. The dance ends and the PRINCE is just about to kiss her hand, when at that moment a clock begins to strike the midnight hour, on which ELLA, with a frightened start, breaks from the PRINCE and runs, leaving him looking after her amazedly. Then his eye falls upon a tiny object on the ground. Picking this up he examines it, lifts it high, in triumph, showing it to be one of ELLA'S slippers. Darkness falls. The midnight striking of the palace clock is taken up by innumerable others: cuckoo, cathedral chimes, and clocks of the common variety. As this chorus ends a ray of moonlight lights the cottage. The fire has nearly dead, and ELLA, in her humble garments, sleeps beside it. She wakens and looks about her.

ELLA. *(Half awake.)* Midnight! Oh, what an escape! Last night I remembered in time to leave, and the night of the day before yesterday. But tonight just as he was about to kiss my hand the Prince...Silly Ella! You have been dreaming. You with a fairy godmother, a pumpkin coach, six cream-white steeds, and a squirrel coachman! You with the most beautiful clothes in the world! You the chosen partner of the Prince! Yonder is poor father's prize pumpkin. And, without, the field-mice are scuttling to their hiding-places, and the big squirrel is scolding the little squirrel for disturbing him, and here am I, the kitchen-drudge, with the fire nearly out! *(She mends the fire.)* Ah, me. 'Twas but a dream! And yet what happiness such dreams bring, while they last! *(The flame flares up, and by its light she sees an object on the floor.)* What's this? One of my dancing-slippers! In my dream there was pitch upon the ground, and one slipper stuck to it, and came off as I was hurrying to my coach. Then what if the dream be true! *(A coach is heard approaching, then stopping at the door. There are voices without. ELLA hides the slipper, as her stepmother and stepsisters enter.)* Madam, young ladies, you enjoyed yourselves, I trust?

GOODWIFE. *(Sharply.)* Don't talk to me. Here, take my wraps!

VAINBETTY. Cendrillon, come and unpin my hair. And don't tug it!

SCRATCHCATTY. Here, come unlace me. I'm suffocating!

(ELLA runs from one to another, assisting them. The GOODMAN enters with a lantern.)

GOODMAN. Well, and so the great ball is over! *(ELLA takes the lantern from him and puts it to its place.)* Were you not lonely in our absence?

ELLA. Lonely? Oh, Father, no! I never had a happier time. The music, the fountains, the dainties to eat and drink, the dancing, the guests, the courtiers and the Prince. I wish it might have lasted forever!

GOODWIFE. What's all this?

Plays for Children

GOODMAN. *(Laughing indulgently.)* Just a young girl's dream

GOODWIFE. She has no business with such dreams, a kitchen-wench, as she is!

VAINBETTY. I should say not, little scullion!

SCRATCHCATTY. Ash-heap girl!

GOODMAN. *(To his wife.)* At any rate I trust you are cured of your royal ambitions. Mother-in-law to the future king; eh, Goodwife? Ha, ha!

GOODWIFE. *(Angrily.)* If you laugh at me I'll turn you out of the house! So there!

VAINBETTY. I was getting on with him swimmingly, till that stranger appeared, sweeping all before her

SCRATCHCATTY. He was just about to declare himself to me, when that stranger appeared.

VAINBETTY. Declare himself to you? Ha!

SCRATCHCATTY. Did you think he was about to declare himself to you? Ha!

GOODMAN. Tut, tut! No one had a chance with that strange lady in the world. Strange, we call her? To me she looked as natural as the day. All petty ambitions and animosities melted before her wholesome goodness, like clouds and darkness before the radiant dawn.

GOODWIFE. Oh, stop your rhapsodizing, and get to bed!

ELLA. What was her name, Father this lady's name?

GOODMAN. Oddly enough, child, that of your mother before you, and your own: Ella.

(He turns out the light and goes into his room.)

ELLA. *(Echoes, softly.)* Ella. The Lady Ella.

GOODWIFE. *(Going into her room.)* Ella. But don't dream you are in her shoes, you Cinderella, you!

VAINBETTY and **SCRATCHCATTY**. *(Also going into their room.)* Ha, ha! That ash-heap queen in the shoes of the Lady Ella!

ELLA. *(Lying down again before the fire, slipper in hand.)* Ella. The Lady Ella.

(The fire dies. Darkness reigns.)

Scene 3

The next morning. Daylight creeps into the room, brightening gradually. The HERALD'S trumpet is heard without, then there is a knock at the door. ELLA wakens, and rises. The others come from their rooms in dressing-gowns, night-caps, curl-papers.)

HERALD. *(Outside.)* Open in the name of King Pomposity the Twenty-Seventh.

GOODWIFE. *(Excited.)* The King's Herald, here! Girls, take your hair out of curl-papers!

VAINBETTY. The dear Prince has sent to inquire how we rested.

SCRATCHCATTY. Ah, they have discovered that strange beauty to be an adventuress, no doubt!

(The HERALD knocks again.)

GOODMAN. *(Yawning, drawing on his coat.)* Coming, coming! Loyalty is loyal, but sleepy, that's all! *(Opens.)* God save the king.

HERALD. *(Entering.)* Now hearken to the royal will and pleasure *(Unfolds a scroll.)* "Whereas..." Hm, hm!

PRINCE AFFABILITY. *(Enters.)* Whereas —

HERALD. The Prince! His Royal Highness the Prince Affability!

(All making low reverences. The women hastily seek to straighten their dishevelment.)

PRINCE. Whereas, a beautiful unknown graced my ball, vanishing each night on the stroke of twelve named Lady Ella. Seeking to trace her to her home, on the third night I caused pitch to be spread on her pathway. To this one tiny dancing-slipper stuck!

(He holds up ELLA'S slipper.)

HERALD. *(Trying to read from scroll.)* "Accordingly, know all men by these presents and more particularly all women..."

PRINCE. The owner of this slipper owns my heart. Her only will I wed.

HERALD. *(Trying to read.)* "Therefore..."

PRINCE. I go from house to house, from castle to cottage, throughout my father's realm...

HERALD. "...wherever are marriageable young according to the latest census..."

PRINCE. ...seeking the owner of this slipper, for my bride.

Plays for Children

GOODWIFE. Your Royal Highness need seek no further. Here she stands. Stand back, Scratchcatty. The older first. Vainbetty, who appeared as the Lady Ella at your ball.

(She presents VAINBETTY.)

PRINCE. *(Bows low, but looks doubtful.)* Ah, Mistress Vainbetty. I hardly think, however, that she is she. I mean the she I seek.

GOODWIFE. I assure you, sir, 'tis she and no other wore that slipper.

PRINCE. Let her prove it, try it on.

VAINBETTY. *(To her mother, whispering.)* I can never cram my foot into that!

GOODWIFE. *(Seizing the shoe and shoving VAINBETTY'S foot into it.)* Here! I'll make it fit.

(VAINBETTY muffles a scream from the pain.)

HERALD. A tight squeeze, but, yes, it fits.

GOODWIFE. You see?

VAINBETTY. *(Sticking her foot out.)* You see?

PRINCE. I — I suppose I see. Perhaps 'tis not to be expected that ladies should look their best in the morning, eh? Let the Ladies-in-Waiting array Mistress Vainbetty for the marriage ceremony.

VAINBETTY. I hope to goodness the ceremony will be a short one. I can't stand the pain of this much longer.

GOODWIFE. Smile, my child. Look pleasant, till you're married. Then you can behave as you please! Prince, behold your bride!

PRINCE. *(Offers VAINBETTY his hand.)* Permit me, Mistress.

DAME TRULY. *(Entering.)* Why, the Princess-to-be has only one shoe on.

VAINBETTY. We shall pick up the other by the way. Good-bye Mother, Sister. I daresay I shall see you some day at the court.

(Trumpets sound. VAINBETTY hobbles out with the PRINCE and HERALD following. They others watch them through the open door.)

SCRATCHCATTY. *(Derisively.)* Vainbetty never can go through with it! Ha, ha! How she limps!

(Suddenly there is a commotion outside. VAINBETTY, who is crying, re-enters with the PRINCE and HERALD.)

PRINCE. There has been some deception here. This is not the owner of the slipper.

VAINBETTY. *(Moaning, removes the slipper.)* Oh, I confess everything. I cannot stand the pain any longer. Here, Prince, here's your slipper.

ELLA. *(Going to her aid.)* Poor Vainbetty. I will get some soothing ointment for your foot.

GOODWIFE. Forgive me, Prince. It was my desire to see my elder daughter married first. But here stands the real owner of the slipper, Scratchcatty, who appeared as Lady Ella at your ball.

PRINCE. Let her prove it, try the slipper on.

SCRATCHCATTY. I never can cram my foot into it!

GOODWIFE. Here. *(After much effort, she gets the shoe on.)* Now, gentlemen. You see?

SCRATCHCATTY. *(Sticking her foot out.)* You see!

PRINCE. *(Sighing.)* I see. Array the future Princess for the marriage ceremony!

SCRATCHCATTY. Good-bye Mother, and Sister. I daresay I shall see you at the palace on visitors' days. Now, Prince, let us be trotting!

(Trumpets sound, and the procession starts as before. Again, a commotion outside. They return.)

SCRATCHCATTY. *(Entering, hopping about, moans with pain.)* I confess! I confess everything! Prince, take your slipper.

ELLA. *(Going to her aid.)* There, there. Poor Scratchcatty. Here's some soothing ointment for you too.

PRINCE. *(To HERALD, preparing to depart.)* Where do we seek now? For seek I will, until I find the true owner of this slipper and my heart.

HERALD. There is still a marriageable daughter in this house, your Royal Highness, according to the latest census.

GOODWIFE. Nothing of the sort.

PRINCE. Where is this other daughter?

GOODWIFE. I tell you, there is no other! There's only the kitchen-wench, a mere scullion. A nobody! *(To her husband who is trying to protest.)* Now don't you contradict me! I shall never hold up my head at Mother's Aid Society, if this gets known! There's no one here but Cinderella. Why don't you support me? *(To her daughters.)* Tell them she's only the ash-heap sifter, Cinderella.

Plays for Children

VAINBETTY. I can't. My toe hurts me so, and she has been so kind.

SCRATCHCATTY. I can't. My heel hurts me so, and she has been so kind.

DAME TRULY. *(Entering.)* Come, come. I want my coffee.

PRINCE. *(Looking at her in surprise.)* Auntie! What are you doing here?

DAME TRULY. Looking after my god-daughter, daughter of the Goodman here, and of his first and more agreeable wife, my niece, Ella.

PRINCE. *(Dreamily.)* Ella. The Lady Ella! My heart told me I should find her here. And yet —

DAME TRULY. Better use your eyes, my dear Affability. Where's the mate to that slipper, Ella?

ELLA. *(Takes it from its hiding place.)* Here, godmother.

(She looks with bashful pleasure, at the PRINCE.)

PRINCE. *(Catching sight of ELLA for the first time.)* It is — it is she! Oh, my Lady!

> *(Advances toward her, places her in a chair, removes her old shoes, and fits on the dancing-slippers, amid general delight which only the GOODWIFE does not share in. Meanwhile the birds are singing as the PRINCE and ELLA start dancing. The lights fade then rise again, disclosing ELLA, now in bridal array, standing with the PRINCE, the others grouped about. Only the GOODWIFE sits apart, on the hearth, the cinder-sifter on her head, trying to peel the pumpkin.)*

End of Play

Plays for Children

SNOW-WHITE AND ROSE-RED

by E. Harcourt Williams

Characters

The Story Teller
Snow-White
Rose-Red
Their Mother
The Dwarf
The Bear Teddie

(Enter the STORYTELLER.)

STORYTELLER. Once upon a time there was a poor widow who lived in a lonely little cottage. In front of the cottage was a garden where two rose-trees bloomed, one of which bore a white rose and the other a red. Now, the widow had two children who were like the rose-trees, for one was called Snow-White and the other Rose-Red.

The two children loved each other so dearly that whenever they went out together they walked hand in hand. Very often they went out into the wood by themselves to pick berries, but the wild beasts never harmed them. If they happened to stay too long in the wood and night came on they just lay down side by side upon the moss and slept until the morning dawned, and as the mother knew this she was never troubled about them.

Once when they had spent the night in the wood and the sunrise awoke them they saw a beautiful child in a shining white robe sitting beside their resting-place. He rose and smiled, said not a word, and went away into the wood.

When they looked round they found they had been lying close to a precipice over which they must have fallen in the darkness if they

Plays for Children

had taken another step. And their mother told them that the child they had seen must have been the little guardian who watches over the children of the world. They all lived a very happy life together in their little cottage in the wood. In the evenings the mother would say—

(The curtain parts and discover the interior of the cottage.)

MOTHER. Now, Snow-White, bolt the door, and do you, Rose-Red, bring me the big fairy tale book, and I will read to you while you eat your suppers.

ROSE-RED. Here is the book, Mummy.

SNOW-WHITE. *(Who has bolted the door.)* And here are your spectacles.

MOTHER. And here are two bowls of porridge for my rosebuds.

ROSE-RED. *(Giving food to the dove that is on a perch by the fire.)* There, Ringy-dove, is your corn, but mind you don't eat it until the morning, because it isn't your supper, it's your breakfast.

SNOW-WHITE. Lambkin shall have some of my porridge presently. *(The face of the DWARF appears at the window.)* Oh, Mother, who is that at the window?

ROSE-RED. It's that wicked old dwarf we saw in the wood to-day. Shall I stamp my foot at him?

SNOW-WHITE. He may be hungry.

ROSE-RED. He deserves to be. He was very ungrateful this afternoon.

MOTHER. Draw the curtains, then perhaps he will go away.

ROSE-RED. There he goes across the snow. How the two rosetrees glitter in the moonlight.

(She draws the curtains.)

MOTHER. Tell me, Rosebud, about the dwarf. You make me anxious.

ROSE-RED. Well, we went into the town, as you know, to buy needles and thread.

SNOW-WHITE. And honey and bread—

ROSE-RED. And ribbons and lace—

SNOW-WHITE. And nutmeg and mace—

(They count these on their fingers.)

ROSE-RED. When we were coming back we saw a huge bird.

SNOW-WHITE. Ever so much huger than our Ringy-dove.

Plays for Children

MOTHER. It must have been an eagle.

ROSE-RED. Well. Suddenly it dived down behind a rock and we heard a piercing shriek.

SNOW-WHITE. I was so frightened.

ROSE-RED. I wasn't.

MOTH4ER. What did you do?

ROSE-RED. We hurried up and found that the eagle had clawed hold of a little dwarf man and was trying to fly away with him.

SNOW-WHITE. So we clawed hold of the dwarfs coat tails and pulled—ever so hard.

ROSE-RED. And I made a noise—you know—a frightening noise—and—and the eagle let go.

SNOW-WHITE. And flew away.

ROSE-RED. Then, if you please, as soon as the dwarf had recovered from his fright he began to scold us and blame us for tearing his beautiful coat tails.

SNOW-WHITE. They weren't beautiful at all.

ROSE-RED. When we had saved him from the big bird.

SNOW-WHITE. And he never even said "Thank you."

ROSE-RED. Wasn't he rude?

MOTHER. What a strange adventure. Is that all?

ROSE-RED. Yes.

SNOW-WHITE. No, you are forgetting the jewels.

ROSE-RED. Oh yes. The dwarf took up a bag full of glittering things before he scampered away.

MOTHER. Well, as you've told me such a fine story to-night perhaps I needn't read to you after all.

ROSE-RED and **SNOW-WHITE.** *(Speaking together.)* Oh! Mummy dear. You must read. How can you be so unkind. Please.

MOTHER. Well then, just one tiny story.

ROSE-RED. Not so very tiny.

SNOW-WHITE. Hush!

Plays for Children

MOTHER. Once upon a time— *(There is a loud knock.)* Quick, Rose-Red, open the door. Very likely some poor wanderer has come to seek shelter.

ROSE-RED. It might be the dwarf.

MOTHER. He would not dare to come to the door.

(ROSE-RED opens the door. BEAR puts his head in. ROSE-RED cries out. SNOW-WHITE hides in the four poster bed.)

BEAR. Don't be afraid, my children. I would not hurt a fly. I am a most gentle sweet bear—a kind of honey bear. I only want to warm myself a little. I am half frozen with the cold.

MOTHER. Poor fellow! Lie down by the fire, but mind you don't burn your thick fur coat or I shall scold you. Come, children, welcome our visitor. You need not be afraid. He is an honest and respectable bear.

(The girls come from their hiding-place.)

BEAR. That's better. Now, won't you brush the snow from my fur coat?

(They fetch the broom and brush him. They gather courage and become gayer during the process.)

SNOW-WHITE. There! Not a single flake is left.

ROSE-RED. Yes, here's one on his back. Roll over, sir.

BEAR. *(Rolling over.)* Ugh!

MOTHER. Now, children, you must eat up your suppers.

BEAR. Supper! Supper! *(Sniffs.)* Ah, I can smell it.

SNOW-WHITE. Will you have some out of my bowl?

ROSE-RED. No, out of mine, out of mine.

BEAR. I will take a little out of each.

(He does so.)

SNOW-WHITE. Now, let's have a game.

BEAR. I don't know any games.

ROSE-RED. Fancy not knowing any games.

MOTHER. He's only pretending.

ROSE-RED. Let's have a romp.

BEAR. Oh, I'm too stiff to romp.

SNOW-WHITE. I've got to be the mother and you've got to be the naughty children.

ROSE-RED. No, you've not got to be the mother. Bear must be the mother. Here's a cap for him.

SNOW-WHITE. And here's an apron.

(They dress him up grotesquely.)

ROSE-RED. There, that's right.

SNOW-WHITE. And now you have to pretend we've got to go to bed and we won't.

ROSE-RED. No, that's a silly game. Mother might remember what the time is.

SNOW-WHITE. Well, then let's make big bear be a horse.

ROSE-RED. Oh yes, and we'll both get on at once.

BEAR. Don't kill me quite, you two.

ROSE-RED. Gee up now, Mr. Bear.

(They both climb on his back and he takes them on an adventurous ride round the room amidst cheers and noises.)

MOTHER. Bedtime! Real!

SNOW-WHITE. No!

ROSE-RED. There! I said that would happen!

BEAR. Roses must sleep o' nights.

SNOW-WHITE. And must poor Bear go out into the cold and snow?

MOTHER. No, if he likes he can sleep here beside the hearth.

(BEAR runts and rubs himself against the Mother.)

ROSE-RED. Look! He's thanking mother.

MOTHER. Now, say good night.

SNOW-WHITE. Good night, dear Bear.

ROSE-RED. Good night, Honey Bear.

BEAR. Good night, Sweetbriers.

(He hugs them both and they go.)

MOTHER. Sleep well, good Bear.

Plays for Children

(She takes the light. The BEAR stretches himself by firelight glow and grunts contentedly. The curtains close and the STORYTELLER reappears.)

STORYTELLER. As soon as morning dawned the two children opened the door and the bear trotted away across the snow and was lost to sight in the wood. But from that day he came to them every night at the same time, laid himself down beside the hearth, and let the children play with him as they liked, and they soon grew so accustomed to him that they never thought of bolting the door until their black friend had arrived.

One morning, when spring came and the whole world was fresh and green, the bear told Snow-White that he would not be able to visit them again all through the summer.

"Where are you going to, dear Bear?" asked Snow-White.

"To guard my treasures from the wicked dwarf," said the Bear.

In the winter, when the ground is frozen hard, he cannot work his way through, and is obliged to stay below in his cave, but now that the warm sun has thawed the earth, he will soon break through it and steal what he can find, and that which once goes into his cave seldom comes out again."

Snow-White grieved sadly over the parting. As she unbolted the door and the bear trotted through, a piece of his coat caught on the latch and was torn off, and it seemed to Snow-White that she saw a glimmer of gold beneath it, but she was not sure. The bear ran quickly away, and soon disappeared behind the trees.

Some time afterwards the mother sent the children into the wood to gather sticks.

(The curtains part and discover the Wood.)

ROSE-RED. See what a fine bundle of wood I've found!

SNOW-WHITE. I wish I were clever like you, Rose-Red. I never can find anything.

ROSE-RED. Goosey Gander! You'll find something wonderful one day, I expect, while I shall be still chopping wood.

SNOW-WHITE. What is that strange thing over there bobbing up and down?

ROSE-RED. Could it be a bunny?

SNOW-WHITE. It's more like a squirrel.

Plays for Children

ROSE-RED. Or a dog jumping about on the end of a string.

SNOW-WHITE. But it's got a long white beard!

ROSE-RED. Why, it is the dwarf!

SNOW-WHITE. So it is the dwarf, and he's caught his beard in the log of the tree.

DWARF. Why do you stand staring there instead of coming to help me?

ROSE-RED. What have you been doing, little man?

DWARF. You silly, prying goose, if you must know, I was splitting the tree to get some small pieces of wood for the kitchen. The large logs which you use would burn up our food in no time. We don't need to cook such a quantity as you great, greedy folk. I had just driven the wedge firmly in and everything seemed right enough, when it slipped on the smooth wood, and popped out, so that the tree closed up in a second, catching my beautiful white beard as it did so; and now I cannot get it out again, and you foolish, milkfaced creature, stand and laugh at me. Oh, how stupid you are!

ROSE-RED. Let's see if we can pull it out. Come along, Snow-White and help me.

SNOW-WHITE. *(They pull.)* Oh, Oh, Oh! It won't move.

ROSE-RED. I know. I will run and fetch some to help.

DWARF. You stupid thing. Why go and fetch others when you are two too many already? Can't you think of something better than that?

SNOW-WHITE. Don't be so impatient! I know what to do. I have got my scissors with me.

ROSE-RED. Yes, yes! The scissors! Who's the clever one now, Snow-White?

SNOW-WHITE. Snip! Snip! There! Now you're free.

DWARF. *(Dancing about with rage.)* Oh, my beautiful beard, my beautiful beard! What clumsy folk to be sure—to cut off a piece of my beautiful beard! Bad luck to you. Oh, my beautiful beard, my beautiful beard!

(He dances off in a fury.)

SNOW-WHITE. Well!

ROSE-RED. He has gone off again without saying "Thank you!"

SNOW-WHITE. Aren't his manners awful!

Plays for Children

DWARF. *(Coming back.)* Tut, tut! What on earth are you stopping here for. Why don't you go away? What a bother you children are to be sure. You flustered me so by cutting my beard that I quite forgot my fishing line. *(He begins to pull line in.)*

ROSE-RED. I wonder what he is trying to catch.

DWARF. I'm in luck, I'm in luck. I've caught a fish as big as a duck. A very fine fish to put on a dish.

SNOW-WHITE. What fun! What fun!

(The DWARF begins to hop about frantically.)

ROSE-RED. What are you doing now? Surely you don't want to jump into the water?

DWARF. I'm not quite such an idiot as that. Can't you see that the silly line has got entangled in my beard and the horrid fish is pulling me in? Oh! Oh! I'm slipping—I'm not strong enough—Oh!—Oh!—I shall be drowned.

SNOW-WHITE. Hold him fast while I try to untangle the knots.

ROSE-RED. *(Holding the DWARF round the waist.)* Can you do it?

SNOW-WHITE. No, I can't. I shall have to snip off just a little piece more—just ever so little. *(Takes out scissors.)* Snip. Snip.

DWARF. *(Yells.)* Idiots! Is it good manners to spoil a person's face like that? You toads! Not content with having shortened my beard, you must now cut the best part out of it. May you go barefoot all the days of your life for your pains! *(He seizes a bag of pearls.)* I'll punish you—you white faced vixen—I'll take you a prisoner to my cave under the ground.

ROSE-RED. Run away, Snow-White, I will hold him. Oh, I wish mother were here!

SNOW-WHITE. She's coming. I know she must be coming.

DWARF. Let me get at her.

ROSE-RED. I can't hold him any longer.

(The DWARF breaks away and goes towards SNOW-WHITE. The BEAR enters growling ominously and intercepts the DWARF.)

DWARF. *(Kneeling in terror.)* Dear Mr. Bear, spare me, I pray you, and I will give you all my treasures. Look at these pearls and precious stones. They shall be all yours if only you will spare my life. I am such a little fellow. You would scarcely feel me between your teeth,

Plays for Children

but here are these two wicked girls—take them and eat them—you will find them tender morsels and as fat as quails.

BEAR. *(With a growl he knocks the DWARF over. He falls behind the trunk.)* Snow-White! Rose-Red! Do not be afraid. I am your own bear. If you will wait for me I will come with you. *(The BEAR'S coat slips off and discovers a Prince in shining gold.)* I am a King's son and I was condemned by that wicked dwarf, who had stolen 'all my treasures, to become a bear and run wild in the woods, but now he has received his well earned punishment and I am released from his spell.

MOTHER. *(Running on.)* My roses—my roses. I knew that you wanted me. What has happened? *(Seeing PRINCE.)* Oh, my sovereign Prince!

PRINCE. No, not your Prince—your son. For I want Snow-White to be my Princess if she will.

SNOW-WHITE. A real Princess!

ROSE-RED. Oh, Snow-White, say you will. I said you would be wonderful!

SNOW-WHITE. *(To ROSE-RED.)* But I couldn't leave you!

PRINCE. No. I have a brother who will guard Rose—Red, and we will all live in a beautiful Palace and share all the wonderful treasures that the dwarf has hidden in his cave.

ROSE-RED and **SNOW-WHITE.** Mother must come too!

PRINCE. Of course, mother must come too.

MOTHER. And I will take my two rose-trees and plant them in the garden and they will be covered with the most beautiful red and white roses that ever were seen.

(A dance.)

Curtain

End of Play

Plays for Children

Plays for Children

ALI BABA

by Wadeeha Atiyeh

Characters

Ali Baba, a woodcutter
Hud-Hud, his donkey
Foomeeya, his wife
Hassan, his son
Khazzim, his brother
Morjana, a slave girl
Buzaid, the chief of the robbers
Kuz-Kuz, a robber
Bou-Loos, another robber
Toos, another robber

Scene 1
Outside Ali Baba's house

Scene 2
Along a road beside a large cave, later that afternoon

Scene 3
Outside the cave, the next morning

Scene 4
The house of Ali Baba., later that day

Plays for Children

Scene 1

Outside Ali Baba's house.

ALI BABA is asleep and snoring under a tree. He looks up, smiles sweetly, nods drowsily and falls asleep again. HUD-HUD, his camel, opens his mouth in a great yawn and then goes back to sleep. A voice inside house shrieks.)

FOOMEEYA. *(Off.)* Oh Ali BBbbaa-a-bbbbaa! *(Pause.)* Ali BBBBAAa-bbbbbaaa! Are you asleep again?

(FOOMEEYA, ALI BABA'S wife, comes out of the house, looking with great disapproval.)

FOOMEEYA. O worthless husband! Rise and go to work! Rise, Oh Sluggard! Is this the time to nap and be lazy? Must we starve to death? We have only a few lentils and a bit of oil left in the house. Rise! Wake! Move! Bestir yourself! Thou art getting fat. *(Pokes him in the stomach. He giggles and promptly goes back to sleep. Exasperated, she goes to HUD-HUD and kicks him. He opens one eye for a moment, cuddles into a more comfortable position and also goes back to sleep.)* Hmm! Truly is it said. "A donkey is a donkey...Whether ye say yea or ye say nay...A donkey remains a donkey!" *(Going back to ALI BABA, becoming more furious.)* But YOU! You are a man! Rise! Move!

(ALI BABA, in a sweet, gentle manner only opens his eyes long enough to say:)

ALI BABA. *(Very slowly.)* Oh woman...how fussy you are. Calm yourself...Rest...Sleep...

(He falls asleep again.)

FOOMEEYA. O Merciful! Is there none to pity me? What shall I do? *(Suddenly she stops, remembering.)* Oh Ali Baba! Today is the day you must pay your brother the debt we owe him. Bestir yourself and take care of it at once.

ALI BABA. Slacken your pace, Woman. Give me time to think.

FOOMEEYA. Time to think? This matter needs *action*! You know he will not wait where money is concerned, even though you are his own brother. He disapproves of you enough as it is. Would that I had never thought to borrow from him. Rise, Ali Baba, and...

(But he has gone back to sleep. Exasperated, she starts to cry but stops suddenly, smiles as one with a new idea, says. "Ah!" and then marches into the house. Immediately she returns carrying a big red pepper in one hand. In her other hand she carries two bowls half full of food one on top of other. She places bowls on table, her eyes glued on pepper. It has been cut in two, though

Plays for Children

she holds it together as one whole pepper. Now she opens it and very carefully, gingerly, puts it to the tip of her tongue. She starts, hangs out her tongue and fans it with her hand, indicating it is burned.)

FOOMEEYA. Oh, it is a very hot pepper! It will serve my purpose well. And perhaps kindle a fire under my dear slow husband. *(To pepper.)* Do your work well, O Red-Hot-Pepper! *(She proceeds to cut up pepper into bowl, then places it beside donkey. In sarcastic, wheedling tones:)* Eat, O Light-of-my-Eyes and Delight-of-my-Heart! (I hope he chokes!) Eat, O Peacock-of-the-World and Light-of-the-Morning! (May he burst!)

(She leaves bowl beside HUD-HUD. He opens his eye, shows interest in the food. She passes the other bowl under ALI BABA'S nose. He smiles as he smells it and languidly reaches for it but she carries it to the table so that he must rise to get it. She goes into house for a moment. As she disappears, HUD-HUD begins to eat from his bowl. Suddenly he jumps as if shot, makes a great noise, and gallops madly in a circle round and round the courtyard. ALI BABA looks up in mild surprise, smiles sweetly and then ignores him. He is interested in food. He looks at bowl on table but too lazy to go to it, he reaches for HUD-HUD'S bowl and begins to eat. Immediately he jumps up, his tongue hanging out, and panting and howling, he too runs round and round the courtyard, a few feet behind HUD-HUD.)

ALI BABA. Hot pepper! Water! Bring water! I am burning! Ouuuooo! Hurry! Water! Ahhhhhh!

(FOOMEEYA re-appears and is pleased her scheme has worked so well. She watches with delight.)

FOOMEEYA. *(Laughing.)* What an active husband have I! Now he is going to the forest with such speed. Good! Then he will chop much wood. Good!

ALI BABA. *(Still running and panting.)* Water! What have you done? Water! Bring water!

FOOMEEYA. *(Still laughing and enjoying it all.)* Now, my husband, perhaps you will continue in this same speed to the forest and go to work. Eh?

ALI BABA. Water! I burn! O why did I marry a wife? Water! Why did I ever look at a woman! Water! Ahh!

FOOMEEYA. And perhaps you will chop wood so fast we shall be rich!

(At this moment she absently picks up bowl and eats from it. Then the big smile on her face changes quickly to amazement as she begins to feel her mouth burning. Shrieking, she too starts running round and round the

159

Plays for Children

courtyard after HUD-HUD and ALI BABA until finally they all fall in one heap, exhausted. Enter HASSAN, the son of Ali Baba.)

HASSAN. Father! Mother! What is happening?

BOTH. Water! Water! *(Still panting and puffing.)*

(HASSAN runs into house, rushes back with a terra-cotta jar and quickly gives them, each some water.)

HASSAN. What have you been eating? Drink! Drink deeply. This will ease your pain. *(He goes from one to the other, giving water. He looks around to see what caused all this, puzzled. FOOMEEYA tries to rise but as he tries to help her to her feet there is a loud knock at the gate. She falls back.)* Oh, father, that is Uncle Khazzim. He is coming to collect the debt. That's what I was rushing to tell you. *(Shouting.)* Enter! Enter!

(He goes to open gate. KHAZZIM, the pompous brother of ALI BABA enters followed by his slave girl, MORJANA. She carries a cushion and a palm leaf. She stops by the door. HASSAN salaams.)

HASSAN. Uncle Khazzim! Welcome.

(But his eyes go to MORJANA and he forgets all else, only repeating with the others the usual polite formula of greeting. HASSAN and MORJANA pantomime in many ways their love for each other. She, with glances and smiles, and he maneuvering to be near her.)

KHAZZIM. Ach! Such vulgar poverty!

FOOMEEYA. *(Embarrassed but tries for dignity.)* O Brother Khazzim, welcome.

ALI BABA. *(Dutifully.)* Allah has favored us with a visit from you, Brother Khazzim.

(KHAZZIM immediately dominates the scene. He strides across courtyard, ignoring everyone, busy with his own importance. He bumps into HUD-HUD, kicks him viciously. HUD-HUD whimpers and runs to ALI BABA who sooths him.)

ALL AT ONCE. Es-salaam aleykom! O Exalted Brother!

(KHAZZIM, his nose in the air, shouts:)

KHAZZIM. Let all mouths close but mine! *(He looks down, suddenly discovering them.)* Why are you all on the floor? Oh, you are all bowing before me. That is right and as it should be. You recognize my high position and my wealth. Commendable! Commendable! *(He catches HASSAN smiling at MORJANA.)* Hassan! On your knees! Humble yourself before your betters!

Plays for Children

(HASSAN kneels but rises immediately and helps his mother to her feet. This time she stays up. Subserviently she rubs her hands together and puts on "manners" though she dislikes KHAZZIM.)

FOOMEEYA. Welcome, O Noble Brother! Our house is honored with your presence.

(KHAZZIM stands tall, looking down his nose at her. HASSAN now helps his father to his feet, but ALI BABA at once looks for a place to sit. He drops on a pile of cushions with great relief.)

ALI BABA. Sit down, Brother, sit and rest. It is good to see your bright countenance. *(To FOOMEEYA.)* Wife, bring refreshment! Honor our guest.

FOOMEEYA. Will it please you to rest here, Brother Khazzim? Do you desire anything? Just command and we shall be as carpets beneath your feet.

(He sits with great ceremony. Then in machine-gun fashion he orders everyone about.)

KHAZZIM. Morjana! Bring more cushions! I wish a refreshing drink! Hassan! Dust my slippers! Morjana! Fan me! There are flies in this courtyard. Eliminate them at once!

MORJANA. Yours to command, mine to obey, master!

(MORJANA quickly moves palm leaf in all directions and then slows down to an even rhythm. She fans him until he rises and then stays on her knees throughout.)

ALI BABA. And how is the state of your health, Brother Khazzim? We hope that your wife is also well and happy?

(HASSAN moves toward MORJANA. KHAZZIM shouts.)

KHAZZIM. Hassan! Go to the Bazaar of Sarkeese, the Merchant, and bring back a package he has readied for me. At once!

HASSAN. But it is the hour of rest now, Uncle Khazzim.

KHAZZIM. Obey at once!

(HASSAN leaves reluctantly. FOOMEEYA returns with a small tray. She serves KHAZZIM and then hovers around him anxious to please. Almost groveling she says:)

FOOMEEYA. O Noble and Exalted Brother! Are you comfortable? We are honored—honored with your presence!

ALI BABA. O Woman! How energetic you are. *(To KHAZZIM.)* I am blessed, O my Brother, with a most active wife. It is very strenuous.

Plays for Children

FOOMEEYA. Action is very much needed.

KHAZZIM. Let all mouths be closed but mine! *(Pause.)* Now! *(Holding out his hand.)* The money!

(ALI BABA hangs his head and is silent.)

FOOMEEYA. Ali Baba, pay your brother!

KHAZZIM. Do not keep me waiting! The money.

FOOMEEYA. Ali Baba, speak. Where is the piece of gold? You put it in your money-belt…

ALI BABA. It is gone.

FOOMEEYA. Gone? It cannot be!

ALI BABA. I—I gave it away.

FOOMEEYA. You gave it away!!

KHAZZIM. *(Ignoring this minor tragedy.)* I am waiting! The money!

FOOMEEYA. But, Ali Baba, to whom did you give it? When? Why?

ALI BABA. Well—it was Suleyman, the beggar at the East Gate. He was in deep trouble—so I gave him the piece of gold. He needed it.

FOOMEEYA. He needed it! What about us? Why didn't you tell me?

ALI BABA. I—I hesitated to disturb your sleep, my good wife. You are quiet so seldom—it seems.

KHAZZIM. Let all mouths be closed but mine! Where is the money? I cannot wait all day. I have more important things to do!

ALI BABA. I am sorry that you are upset, Brother Khazzim, I would be grateful if you would give me a few days to…

KHAZZIM. You are a fool, Ali Baba! Why should I wait for my money? I do not run my business affairs so loosely. Bah! I have always deplored your haphazard ways…

(ALI BABA nods and says "true, true" at intervals throughout sequence.)

FOOMEEYA. Listen to your brother, Ali Baba, and learn!

KHAZZIM. Let all mouths close but mine! *(To ALI BABA.)* Where is your ambition? I find you in this disgraceful poverty…

FOOMEEYA. Don't miss this opportunity to learn, Ali Baba!

KHAZZIM. Let all mouths close but mine! *(To ALI BABA.)* Why don't you go to the Market Place and buy and sell as I do?

FOOMEEYA. Listen to your wise and clever brother…

Plays for Children

KHAZZIM. Let all mouths close but mine! *(To ALI BABA.)* You have no servants to order about, as I do

FOOMEEYA. *(Elated.)* Learn, O Ali Baba, learn!

KHAZZIM. Let all mouths close but mine! *(To ALI BABA.)* You have no robes of silk, as I have! No gold in your storehouse. No storehouse!

ALI BABA. True, true.

KHAZZIM. Bah! Don't expect me to help you. Now, listen to what I say. I will give you until sun-down and if the money is not ready… *(He looks around toward HUD-HUD.)* Why don't we sell this ridiculous donkey!

(At this, HUD-HUD begins to shake all over.)

FOOMEEYA and **ALI BABA.** Oh! No!

KHAZZIM. His hide will bring some money. His hoofs and his carcass could be sold for dog meat!

ALI BABA. Oh, no! Hud-Hud is my friend! I can't sell my friend! *(To HUD-HUD.)* Don't worry, Hud-Hud, I will protect you. We shall be together always. Don't worry. Come, you may help me work out this problem. This needs deep meditation.

(They go and sit under the tree.)

KHAZZIM. Then you had better do something quick. I want that money or the donkey goes! I have spoken!

(FOOMEEYA, at this cruelty, suddenly changes to a terrible anger.)

FOOMEEYA. This donkey is the means of our livelihood! *(Losing all control.)* Son of 60,000 dogs! May your ancestors roast in Ja-han-um! Dragger-of-dead-dogs!

ALI BABA. Gently, Woman, gently.

FOOMEEYA. My husband, thy brother, has wealth. He has real wealth. He has untold wealth—

KHAZZIM. Let all mouths close but m… What did you say about wealth?

(KHAZZIM looks avaricious.)

FOOMEEYA. My husband, thy brother, is a good man, a kind…

KHAZZIM. *(Interrupting.)* But where is this wealth you mention? Ali Baba, are you keeping a secret from me?

163

Plays for Children

ALI BABA. *(Bewildered.)* No—no—I—I—

(FOOMEEYA now realizes the misinterpretation and bursts with laughter.)

FOOMEEYA. Oh! Haha! Hahaha! May Allah give you light! I meant that my husband, thy brother, has the wealth of goodness, of kindness—not of worldly goods.

(But KHAZZIM does not believe and looks at them both suspiciously. He goes to ALI BABA.)

KHAZZIM. You are hiding something from me! You are only pretending that you are poor. Ali Baba, confess!

ALI BABA. But—but—by my beard, I swear I have nothing—

FOOMEEYA. But he has great wealth! And you cannot have any of it!

KHAZZIM. Ali Baba, where is your wealth? I demand to know! *(Changing to a wheedling tone.)* Am I not your own brother, Ali Baba? You must share it with me.

ALI BABA. But—but—I possess nothing.

(FOOMEEYA laughs.)

KHAZZIM. O Unutterable woman! You are gloating! It is you who is hiding the wealth!

(FOOMEEYA becomes sober and decides to be practical.)

FOOMEEYA. This has gone far enough. *(Softening.)* Now go, my husband, to your work. There is so little food in the house, our rich brother would not help us if we were starving! Go, Ali Baba and earn a few pennies. I understand now—I will be satisfied. Go.

(She picks up an axe and lays it in his arms and then gently pushes them both and gets them going. They exit. KHAZZIM still suspicious, follows them to door.)

KHAZZIM. Are you sure they are going only to cut wood.

FOOMEEYA. *(Sarcastically.)* No, he is going to mine opals and dig rubies!

KHAZZIM. I will find out! Woe to you if you are deceiving me! *(Turns to FOOMEEYA with a terrible look.)* You! You she-devil! You have influenced my brother against me! Where is this wealth you are keeping from me?

FOOMEEYA. You are truly blind, O Cruel-and-Greedy-One! I see now. You are only an avaricious and selfish man! Go, fool! We have no wealth as you know it.

(She pushes him out and shuts the door in his face.)

KHAZZIM. *(Off.)* I will find out! I will find out!

(FOOMEEYA turns toward MORJANA. She holds out her hands and raises her to her feet.)

FOOMEEYA. You poor child, what a master you have. He is the most crafty, the most miserly, the most disagreeable—to tell truth, my dear Morjana, thy master stinketh!

MORJANA. *(Very soberly.)* You will allow me, my Lady, to be—of the same opinion?

(The two women look at each other understandingly and then burst out laughing. HASSAN returns, empty-handed.)

HASSAN. Where is Uncle Khazzim? There was no package for him. Sarkcese the Merchant knew nothing about it. There must be a mistake. Will you tell him, Morjana, that…

FOOMEEYA. There is no mistake! Your Uncle sent you away with purpose. I see it clearly now.

(She looks at them with a knowing smile, picks up the tray and goes into house.)

HASSAN. Morjana, what is all this. What has happened?

MORJANA. Oh, it is the game of life, pulling them this way and that way—and they are all disturbed. In short, your Uncle being a "strict" business man—

HASSAN. —and my father an easy man, living in a world of dreams. They cannot understand each other. I know, I know.

MORJANA. Your father has given away the money that was to pay the debt.

HASSAN. He has given it away? *(Groaning.)* Oh! *(Smiling.)* I know. He no doubt explained that someone needed it desperately?

MORJANA. Exactly that! And your Uncle will give him only until sundown to raise the money.

HASSAN. *(Thinking aloud.)* I must find a way. Well, we have until sundown. Perhaps Rashid the Rug-Merchant to whom I am apprenticed would—he might—he might advance me the money.

Plays for Children

MORJANA. And your mother too is disturbed. And poor Hud-Hud. He had a scare.

HASSAN. You are so wise, Morjana— and so beautiful! There is no Morjana but Morjana!

MORJANA. And there is no one like Hassan. But I am only thy Uncle's slave—

HASSAN. To me you are a Princess! Would that I could be your slave. Then you can say, "Let all mouths close but mine!"

MORJANA. *(Laughing.)* "Let all mouths close but mine!"

HASSAN. *(Playing the game with her.)* Yours to command, mine to obey, my Princess!

MORJANA. Bring me cushions! Dust my shoes! Rest your tongue! Fan me! There are flies here! Eliminate them at once!

HASSAN. Yes, your Aloofness! Yes, your Aloofness! Oh, you forgot. "I have spoken!"

MORJANA. "I have spoken!"

HASSAN. *(More seriously.)* —and I would obey your every wish, O Morjana, more than that, I would devote one hour every day to the composing of poetry just to describe you. *(As if beginning.)* Thou art the Fullness-of-light! O Rival-of-the-Moon! O Dawn-upon-the-Land! O Light-of-my-Darkness! O Joy-of-the-Earth! O—

MORJANA. Poets tell such splendid lies! Oh! I must follow my master.

(She flits around and gathers her belongings. HASSAN follows her where ever she goes, stops when she stops, blocking her exit, delaying her departure.)

HASSAN. O most fortunate Uncle!

MORJANA. I must follow my master. I go, Hassan.

(She bows shyly, salaams and leaves. The lights fade.)

Scene 2

Along a road beside a large cave. ALI BABA is again sleeping on the side of the road with HUD-HUD.

Noise offstage. Horsemen coming from a distance. Louder and louder as they approach.

ROBBERS. *(Off.)* Zay-naat ya bu Zu-lof! Hey-hey, hey-hey, hey!

(ALI BABA wakes, and is terrified. He acts quickly. Has time enough only to hide his donkey in a clump of thorn bushes and up the rock he goes.

Plays for Children

The riders are now heard, calling each other, the neighing of horses, much activity. BUZAID, the chief of the robbers, enters, directing the men, still unseen. He is a big man with a black oval beard, just long enough to fringe around his chin. He carries a whip.)

BUZAID. Men! Make haste! *(They appear dragging big leather bags full of loot. BUZAID, with long bold steps, strides to the face of the Rock, raises his arm and cries in a voice of seven thunders.)* OPEN SESAME!

(At these words a great noise is heard and the rock opens, disclosing a huge cavern. It is full of treasure: bales of silk and brocades, gold and silver in heaps, money in leather purses, chests overflowing with jewels, sabers, jeweled swords, curved scimitars. The men rush into the cave, throw down their bulging saddle bags, disappear, and return dragging more bags.)

BUZAID. Are all the bags in, men? *(Calling off.)* Kuz-kuz! Bou-loos!

(They come out of Cave.)

BOU-LOOS. All finished, Chief.

KUZ-KUZ. UM-Mmllll, umrumm-rubmymm, unmishee-eeefffff!

(He tries to talk with his mouth full. He carries a bundle of food. Food sticks out of his belt, pockets, under his fez. He loves to eat and is never seen without food.)

BUZAID. I want this finished before nightfall. This is the biggest haul we have ever made!

(BUZAID opens a bundle he has been carrying and holds up a big pearl in the shape of a pear.)

ALL. *(Admiring it.)* Ma sh'allah!

BOU-LOOS. *(Whistling.)* Ah! Is that a pearl, Chief?

BUZAID. Not in all the world is there a pearl so magnificent, so enormous! And now it is mine! *(Next he holds up a ruby ring.)* Ahhhh! Have you ever seen such a ruby? *(Talking to it.)* "O Ruby, thou art like a drop of blood from the dagger's blade!" *(He gloats.)* And now it is mine! *(Next he pulls out a crown, studded with precious stones, a great emerald in center.)* And—ha, ha! We have the Sultan's very crown! See this emerald? Know that Kings have out bid each other to own it. It is worth a kingdom! And now it is mine! *(He pulls out more jewels and caresses them with great satisfaction. He struggles to tear himself away from them.)* Kuz-Kuz, call that new fellow!

(KUZ-KUZ moves off, eating and mumbling a call, motioning with his arm.)

Plays for Children

KUZ-KUZ. UGlllbbbmm, brvvvgmm-m, icgklsw.zzzsmm, Too- ooo.

(TOOS, the youngest and newest robber enters, eager and excited. He is young and small. He stumbles over a robber's feet and arrives sprawled before the BUZAID. They all laugh at him.)

BUZAID. Hmm. What is your name again, Young-One?

TOOS. My name is Toos, the son of Hamid Bey, Chief.

BUZAID. And of what clan?

TOOS. The clan of Ibn Osman, in the land of Yemen, Sir.

BUZAID. So, you are from the Southern Desert! Good fighters!

TOOS. Oh, yes, Chief!

BUZAID. You may stay and camp with us. You make the fortieth thief to your group. You will develop well with our training. And you may join these men as one of my special lieutenants. You may camp with us. Of course, you understand, O Green-One, that you can never go back. You now know the secret of the Cave. No one who knows the secret has ever left our band alive. Remember that!

(TOOS eagerly nods and shakes his head alternately.)

TOOS. Yes! No! Yes! No! No! Oh, no! Oh, yes, Chief. I have always wanted to be a robber!

(BOU-LOOS slaps him unexpectedly on the back. TOOS jumps, frightened, but tries to act tough. At this point HUD-HUD moves in the bushes and the bells is wears around his neck tinkle. ALI BABA pokes his head, frightened, motions for HUD-HUD to quiet his bells, then quickly disappears.)

BUZAID. What was that?

TOOS. Must be the wind, Chief. *(But eagerly draws sword.)* Shall I?

(All laugh at him. TOOS, still eager, goes to look inside cave, sword drawn and chest puffed. No one pays further attention to him.)

BUZAID. We accumulated a great amount of treasure. Not since we cleaned out the Palace of King Da-Wood have we carried away so much.

KUZ-KUZ. *(Pointing to cave.)* Ummmlplushifff ummrummscklikk Tooos-ooo!

BOU-LOOS. Let us shut the cave on Toos! That should really scare him!

BUZAID. Shut Sesame! *(Cave closes. Soon TOOS is heard yelling to get out. All laugh.)* Open Sesame!

(Rock opens at his command. TOOS comes out scared dragging his sword after him.)

TOOS. WOOOoooooo! How did that happen?

BUZAID. You had better know, Toos, that it is well never to enter the cave alone—unless you have a friend outside. For should the door close, it cannot be opened from inside. Do you understand? *(TOOS nods, but looks frightened still. All laugh. Again tinkle of bells.)* What is that? Draw your swords! Scatter!

(They disperse and search, but find nothing.)

BOU-LOOS. It must be the wind.

(Satisfied, BUZAID then, busies himself tying the bundle of jewels.)

KUZ-KUZ. UMMmmm-mrumm glybubbbbubb.

BOU-LOOS. Say, are you a man or a pig? All the time eat, eat, eat!

(BUZAID cracks whip for attention.)

BUZAID. Make haste, men! We have delayed long enough. This trip should not take long. We go only to meet the rest of the men coming back. *(He raises his arm and pronounces.)* Shut sesame!

(Rock closes with a crash. Great noise accompanies them as they leave. One moment of silence and ALI BABA creeps from his hiding place. In spite of his terror he approaches the cave and tries the magic words.)

ALI BABA. O-o-pen s-s-sesame? *(Rock opens for him too. He falls back in amazement with fright right onto HUD-HUD, who has just come out from the bushes. Both are on the ground looking into cave with awe. They recover and go in. ALI BABA exclaiming:)* Gold! Jewels! Wonderful! Ohh! *(He runs around in cave in great excitement, decking himself with necklaces and sticking swords in his belt. HUD-HUD catches this exciting mood and gallops around smelling the jewels and trying to eat them.)* Oh, no Hud-Hud! You must not eat them! *(HUD-HUD is hurt and slinks away, but ALI BABA cheers him.)* Come, Hud-Hud! Here is a beautiful necklace for you and some jewels for your ears—and you may carry these bags. Won't Foomeeya be pleased! She will not scold us any more, will she, Hud-Hud? No! *(He then loads all that he and HUD-HUD can carry. ALI BABA raises his arm, with confidence now, and commands.)* Shut Sesame!

(They start for home. ALI BABA sings a song to fit his mood and they dance off to the rhythm.)

Plays for Children

BUZAID. *(Entering.)* This is the last trip. Tonight we celebrate! A feast! *(Raises arm.)* Open sesame!

(*Cave opens. They all start in and discover that their treasure is missing.*)

BUZAID. Someone has stolen our stolen goods! We have been discovered!

ALL. No! No!

BUZAID. And if we don't find and eliminate who ever did this, they shall return and we shall lose all the treasure!

BOU-LOOS. The secret is out! But how are we going to find whoever did this?

BUZAID. We have to find him—and at once! Scatter over the city, all of you, and ask questions! Find a man who has had sudden riches! Find him, I tell you! Whatever method you want to use, but find him! Go! Speed! Lose no time! On your way!

(*They all dash off as the lights go to black.*)

Scene 3

Outside the cave, the next morning.

The BUZAID is pacing back and forth.

BUZAID. Where is that Son-of-the-Desert? Toos has disobeyed my orders! And if he is not back soon I shall suspect him of treachery. I should not have trusted him—

BOU-LOOS. He will come back, Chief, I am sure—he wants to be a "great robber."

KUZ-KUZ. Toos is trust-worthy, Chief. He is just giddy with excitement—like a new puppy.

BUZAID. Then why isn't he back? *(Shouting.)* There has been still more taken out of the Cave! Could it be Toos?

BOU-LOOS. No, Chief, not Toos.

BUZAID. Or could it be the accomplice of that man that was in the cave. Why could none of you find him?

BOU-LOOS. I wandered all night, Chief. No sleep—no food. I think tomorrow I can get a bit of information from the cobbler in the Bazaar.

Plays for Children

BUZAID. We cannot wait for any tomorrows! As soon as this Toos fellow reports, I myself shall go...

(*TOOS appears noisily.*)

TOOS. (*Singing.*) Zay-naat ya bu zu-lof! Hey ,hey—Hey, hey—Hey!

BOU-LOOS. Here he is! That is Toos!

KUZ-KUZ. (*Eating.*) Say, Toos, were you supping with the King. Where have you been all this time?

TOOS. (*Ready to burst.*) Chief! Chief! I found him! (*Wildly he begins, stumbling over his words and mixing them all together.*) ...in the third Tantaweel of the hill—on the house of Baba—of the third Ali—by the woman in the third black shawl—in the street of the third hill—

(*BUZAID grasps his shoulder firmly. TOOS makes visible effort to gather his wits.*)

BUZAID. Stop this gibble-gabble, bibble-babble!

TOOS. I have found him!

BUZAID. Tell quickly! Who is he? Where is he! And all else that you know! Tell! Tell!

TOOS. His name is Ali Baba, Chief. And he is a woodcutter. I learned that this Ali Baba had suddenly become rich

BUZAID. That is our man!

BOU-LOOS. By Allah, you are a smart fellow, Toos!

BUZAID. Where does he live?

TOOS. The third house on the hill in the street called Tantaweel.

BUZAID. You have done good work, Toos. (*Slaps him hard on the back.*) There is no doubt at all that you have found the man. Now, we must act quickly! (*He cracks his whip in time with his thoughts.*) Here is the plan, men. Listen! We shall go to the house of this Ali Baba, all of us, and we shall time it when the family is all together at the evening meal. First, we four shall go, but only I will be visible. I shall be an oil merchant on my way from Samarcand. And I will have forty jars of oil in my caravan—ha, ha, ha—there will be one containing oil, true, but each of the others will hold a man! You and you and you and all the others...

ALL. Ohh! Ahh! Ahha! Brilliant! Masterly plan!

BOU-LOOS. A very wise plan, Chief. Sharpen your swords, men!

Plays for Children

BUZAID. Kuz-Kuz, go into that white inlaid chest we brought from Damascus. In it is long white beard. Bring it to me. *(KUZ-KUZ disappears into cave.)* Exactly what I shall need now!

(KUZ-KUZ returns carrying the beard. BUZAID puts it on.)

BUZAID. Bou-Loos now bring me a green turban. *(BOU-LOOS does.)* For when he sees the green head-piece he will think I have made the Pilgrimage to Mecca—and that I am a holy man. Ha, ha, ha!

BOU-LOOS. *(Returning with the head-piece.)* It is a perfect disguise, but is it enough for you and the jars (us) to gain entrance into Ali Baba's house Chief?

BUZAID. No, it is not, but I intend to make sure by using the Bond of Hospitality! That will give us entrance without question.

ALL. Splendid! Great idea!

TOOS. The Bond of Hospitality?

BOU-LOOS. The Bond of Hospitality, Toos, is a custom of this country. It is the custom to shelter and feed any wayfarer who passes by and asks for it.

TOOS. Oh! Of course!

BUZAID. Any wayfarer! Any stranger! What a custom! Hah! We shall certainly make use of it! Now, men. *(Imitating an old man.)* I shall be that wayfarer and I will ask for shelter. And then it will not be difficult to ask that my jars of "precious" oil be taken into the courtyard. *(Straightening up.)* Does everyone understand the instruction? No failures! *(The men mumble assent.)* This will be the signal. Do not act until you receive this signal, not under any circumstances! When the right moment comes, I will go to the jars and I will slap the first jar on the side three times. That man inside will then slap his jar three times, so the next man will hear and he—and so on. Then you will all leap out and—you know what to do. Let us rehearse it. Over there, men!

(They all leap into the air and shout with much flashing of swords as the lights dim.)

Scene 4

The house of Ali Baba. Later that day.

ALI BABA and disguised BUZAID are seated on gorgeous, striped cushions. ALI BABA is richly dressed. On his head is a huge turban and big rings on his finger.

Plays for Children

FOOMEEYA reclines in her shining rich clothes, admiring herself in a long handled mirror. HUD-HUD poses near stairway, sitting up on his hind legs, his two front hoofs crossed complacently in front of him, his head at a very haughty angle.

ALI BABA. My house is honored with your presence, O Noble Merchant.

BUZAID. Your hospitality is most gracious, Kind Host.

(MORJANA enters with a tray, puts two glasses on table before them.)

FOOMEEYA. Morjana! Come and comb my hair. Bring the new perfume—and don't forget the sweetmeats! Make haste!

(MORJANA goes off for a moment and then goes up the stairs to serve her mistress. Soon FOOMEEYA is asleep. Morjana, suspicious, observes below, her gaze going from BUZAID to jars. At this point, two robbers pop their heads from jars and then quickly disappear, but MORJANA doesn't see them.)

ALI BABA. You have travelled far?

BUZAID. From Samarcand. Oil is purest in that land.

ALI BABA. *(Picking up a glass.)* Drink and refresh your heart, Good Merchant. I beg of you to partake also of my food, unworthy of you though it is.

BUZAID. Your generosity is boundless, my good host. I would repay you for your kind hospitality— with a jar of my precious oil. A little gift…

(He rises to go to the jars to give the signal, but MORJANA is alert. In an instant she glides down the stairs almost in one move, and she arrives at the jars just before him, stopping his progress.)

MORJANA. *(Looking at both, salaams.)* Masters, forgive me, but our store of oil is overflowing and we have no room for more. But we are grateful to you for having sent us this great plenty.

(BUZAID has no choice but to go back and sit down. MORJANA sinks to floor beside jars.)

ALI BABA. May your generosity never diminish, Good Merchant, we are grateful. Morjana runs our house with great wisdom. She knows best about such things. She was a slave-girl that belonged to my brother. And she is a jewel!

FOOMEEYA. *(Yawning.)* Oh, how tired I am. I shall nap. Serve our guest some food, Morgana. *(She now comes down and disappears into house,*

Plays for Children

her long veils trailing behind her and still intently looking into hand-mirror. She says as she goes:) Have no one disturb me, Morgana.

BUZAID. The bounty of Allah be yours, I cannot partake of food—just yet.

ALI BABA. But now it grieves me that you will not eat of my food. *(Taking a mouthful.)* Ahhh! Paradise! My Friend, how would you describe Paradise?

BUZAID. Hmm! Oh, there must be palm trees there—and fountains—and pleasant gardens—and rivers flowing—and an inexhaustible amount of sweetmeats—and beautiful maidens having large eyes. And if I find no such things in Paradise when I arrive there—I will leave it for certain!

(MORJANA goes up the stairs.)

ALI BABA. Excellent! Excellent! *(Claps hands in delight.)* You have a sweet tongue, my Friend. But may your life continue on this earth for many more years. Now, I am perfectly content and comfortable here. I have all I desire and more. I possess more gold than I can count! And some of the most beautiful gems—

BUZAID. *(Grinding his teeth.)* And where, my Good Host, do you keep this great amount of treasure? Surely this house is not big enough to hold so much.

ALI BABA. True, true, I have a great abundance now. And how it came about is a very wonderful story! Would you like to hear it, my Friend. It will amuse you—

(The action and story go on simultaneously. ALI BABA goes on talking oblivions of anything wrong going on about him. At an indicated moment BUZAID rises, carefully, so as not to disturb the story and stealthily goes toward jars to give signal. His eyes stay on ALI BABA. He bumps into something. It is HUD-HUD who has strolled to the center and is calmly silting up looking perky. BUZAID starts back to his cushion, but soon sees the path clear again to the jars and takes the opportunity to try again. But, HUD-HUD decides to continue his stroll between the jars, so that they meet and bump again. He gives up in disgust and goes back to his seat to wait for another opportunity.)

ALI BABA. Not long ago I was but a poor wood-cutter. One day I was led to go to work. I obeyed. I went to the forest to cut wood. And in the course of my work I came upon a great wickedness and evil-doings, a den of thieves! It was full of stolen treasure—enough for two Kingdoms! It was the most marvelous accumulation in this world! I wish you could have seen it! I was frightened and at first I wanted to run away, but it was plain that I had to do something. I did. I loaded all that my donkey and I could carry and did the only thing I knew, to be right. I took the treasure back to their owners. First, I went to the King. And oh, that was a wonderful experience. I thought the King was a King—but the King was only a Man. And he was such a nice man. Well, he was so pleased he gave me one-half of the treasures! He said it was a "reward"—for what, I do not know. Then I went to that great and honorable man, the Merchant Mustaffa Pasha. And what do you think he did when I returned what rightfully belonged to him? Yes, he too, gave me one-half of his treasures! *(BUZAID is back, seated now.)* And now, the next thing I must do is to finish taking the rest of the treasures back to their owners as fast as I can. Don't you think so, Good Merchant? Now I know evil can be destroyed.

> *(HUD-HUD decides to investigate jars. ROBBERS pop heads up. HUD-HUD tries to lick their faces. One is frightened. One strikes him.)*

BUZAID. You are confident only because you have much gold now.

ALI BABA. Oh, no, my Friend, I give it away whenever I can.

BUZAID. *(Hits table in anger.)* You give it away?

ALI BABA. Yes.

BUZAID. *(Anger rising.)* You are indeed a simple man! If you will please excuse me—I must see to my caravan—

> *(He rises to go to the jars and give the signal. Enter HASSAN. They collide halfway. HASSAN is now dressed like a Prince, in brocades and satins.)*

HASSAN. *(Salaams.)* Forgive me! Welcome, O Noble Sheykh. Our house is honored with your presence. Your countenance has brightened our home.

ALI BABA. This is my son, Hassan, Good Merchant.

BUZAID. *(Bowing impatiently.)* Good day, Young-One. If you will please allow me, I must see to my caravan.

HASSAN. O Most Honored Guest! Your caravan is well-protected. I have locked all the gates myself. No intruders can possibly enter. Your caravan is as safe as if it were in your own courtyard. Will it please you to rest again?

ALI BABA. True, true, my Friend. All is well. Rest your mind. I see that you are a good merchant. You love your merchandise. Oil is a very precious thing.

BUZAID. *(Furious.)* No! Gold is more precious! And I would deal only in gold and jewels!

ALI BABA. Ah jewels—jewels! As I was telling you, I have some of the most beautiful, gems! I had a pearl a few days ago that was shaped like a perfect pear. I gave it to a young child, a pretty little neighbor, to wear at the end of one of her braids. And I have an emerald that the King gave me from his own crown. Oh, why do I not show you. Would you like to see my collection, my Friend?

BUZAID. *(Bitterly.)* It—would be— a pleasure.

(They rise to go into house. ALI BABA is pleased as a child.)

ALI BABA. And if I can find another emerald as beautiful as the one I have I will have them set at the very tips of my son's wedding slippers! Or, if I can't find another, I shall have this one just cut in two! *(Delighted.)* Won't that be wonderful? *(BUZAID groans.)* Come, my Friend, let me show you. Come and feast your eyes.

BUZAID. *(Trying to look casual.)* I will be happy, of course. But first, let me close that first jar. It looks loose.

(He goes toward jars and is about to raise his hand to slap it for signal, when HUD-HUD calmly slinks from behind like a tractor, so that BUZAID is pushed out of his course and knocked to the floor. Signal is again delayed. ALI BABA helps him up and leads him toward house.)

ALI BABA. Oh! I am so sorry! Forgive! Forgive! *(Scolding HUD-HUD.)* That was not good hospitality, Hud-Hud! For shame! Come, my Friend, let me wipe out this bad experience—let me show you the treasure. They will delight you, I know and you will agree that they are truly magnificent . . .

(As they continue toward house and BUZAID has recovered, HUD-HUD makes a running start and "butts" him with his head. BUZAID looks furiously at him, but HUD-HUD looks innocent hanging his head and crossing his feet in a sorrowful pose. They leave. HUD-HUD struts off. MORJANA comes flying down the stairs.)

MORJANA. Hassan!

HASSAN. Morjana! What is wrong?

MORJANA. Sh-sh! Hassan! That man is not an Oil Merchant! And these jars contain not oil, but men armed with huge knives! This is a plot! *(HASSAN starts toward jars, wildly waving his sword, but she holds him back.)* No, Hassan! Not that way! There are too many! Thirty-six more beyond the wall!

HASSAN. Then I had better call the men for help—

MORJANA. No, no, Hassan! We will have to use our wits.

HASSAN. Of course. But, Morjana, are you sure? How do you know?

MORJANA. I have not time to convince you, Hassan. Trust me, I beg you! But I can tell you this much. I saw heads pop up from these jars!

HASSAN. If I must not raise an alarm what shall we do?

MORJANA. I have a plan. We must work fast. This courtyard is closed and we are closed in with them. I have some oil on the lire and it must be boiling now.

HASSAN. Boiling oil!

MORJANA. There is no other way to save our household, Hassan!

HASSAN. You are right! Very well, you take care of these and I will go beyond the wall and take care of the rest!

(MORJANA runs right. HASSAN runs left. ROBBERS pop lids. HUD-HUD comes on. Tries to lick their faces, but they push him away. MORJANA returns, carrying a huge earthen clipper and creeps upon the unsuspecting robbers. She goes to first jar and before she pours she speaks.)

MORJANA. O thou in the cold jar, sit then in comfort and be warmed, for the night is chill. *(She pours in the oil in. A groan is heard from inside jar. KUZ-KUZ jumps up and runs out. She shows satisfaction as she creeps to the next jar.)* And here is warmth for thy brother— *(Again she pours, and BOU-LOOS runs off screaming. She creeps to next jar.)* Ah! Truly is it said that a cold lodging brings small comfort! Well then, be thou comforted! *(Pours and TOOS jumps out and runs off screaming. HASSAN returns.)* There, that takes care of them.

HASSAN. But now there is still the Robber Chief!

MORJANA. Sh-sh! Let me carry on. Trust me, Hassan. Sit down with them and act as if all is well. And don't be surprised at anything I may do. Only keep him from those jars until I return. Our lives depend on it.

(He nods. She runs off as BUZAID and ALI BABA return.)

ALI BABA. Now, my Friend, tell me, in all your travels have you ever seen such jewels?

BUZAID. *(Furious.)* No, never.

Plays for Children

ALI BABA *(Taking off ring.)* Will it please you to accept this ruby as a little gift from me? I know that every man yearns for a jewel such as this. And it gives me pleasure to fulfill the desires of my friends.

BUZAID. Then you really do give away such expensive presents?

(MORJANA reappears unseen by BUZAID and ALI BABI. She makes her way to one of the jars.)

ALI BABA. *(Enjoying himself.)* Oh, yes! Once a week I gather all my friends and give them gifts. And when I go for a walk I always, carry a pile of little bags full of gold and silver. And I give them away to all whom I meet. To all those walking before me and to all those behind me. To those upon my left and to those upon my right. And all...

(At this BUZAID loses control.)

BUZAID. No wonder! The wealth will soon be gone!

ALI BABA. But it gives pleasure. Isn't that more important? It is not real wealth, my friend.

BUZAID. Not real wealth!

(Now his anger has reached its height. He rises with intent, that nothing will stop him from reaching the jars this time, but MORJANA runs up behind him and crashes the jar over his head. He falls unconscious to the floor.)

MORJANA. Quick tie him up before he comes to.

(HASSAN takes the rope and binds him fast.)

ALI BABA. *(Frightened.)* O wicked girl! What have you done? You have ruined us! O Calamity! Calamity!

HASSAN. Father! It was to preserve you, not ruin you! Listen. He was your enemy! He is not an Oil Merchant—he is the Robber Chief!

ALI BABA. The Robber Chief?

MORJANA. Yes—he came to do you harm.

ALI BABA. Oh, no, that cannot be!

MORJANA. He is only disguised as an oil merchant! Look!

(She pulls off the long white beard of BUZAID, who is flat on the floor, and reveals the short black one. ALI BABA stands horrified.)

ALI BABA. Yes, that is the robber chief I saw!

HASSAN. And the forty jars contained not oil, but robbers! Morgana has put an end to their evil and wickedness! It was her plan, father.

Plays for Children

ALI BABA. *(Recovering.)* Then you have saved my life! O courageous girl! But how did you discover all this?

MORJANA. *(In mock humility.)* Master, a woman is a woman.

ALI BABA. You shall never call me "master" again! I give you your freedom! You are no longer a slave, Morjana!

(She sinks to her knees.)

HASSAN. There is no Morjana but Morjana!

ALI BABA. Rise, my child, we are all equal. And in addition—you shall marry my beloved son Hassan! *(ALI BABA claps his hands.)* Prepare a Wedding Feast at once! And let it last forty days and forty nights!

(There is great excitement and hustle and bustle as the lights dim on the happy scene.)

End of Play

CPSIA information can be obtained at www.ICGtesting.com
Printed in the USA
LVOW10s1636230216

476356LV00003B/683/P